Going Home...

RENTING TO HOME OWNERSHIP IN 10 EASY STEPS

ഇൻൽ

Michael Delaware

If, And or But
Publishing Company

Published by
'If, And or But' Publishing Company
P.O. Box 2559
Battle Creek, Michigan 49016 USA
www.ifandorbutpublishing.com
ISBN-13: 978-0615928722 (If, And or But Publishing)
ISBN-10: 0615928722

This book also contains clipart illustrations which were acquired by means of royalty free usage rights in 2013 and are copyright to: GraphicsFactory.com on pages: 1, 3, 9, 23, 25, 55, 56, 77, 95, 99, 113, 133, 147, 157, 159 & 165. All other illustrations are copyright to *If, And or But Publishing.*

While attempts have been made to verify all information provided in this publication; neither the author nor the publisher assumes any responsibility for errors, omissions, or contrary interpretations of the subject matter herein. The views expressed are those of the author alone, and should not be taken as expert instruction or commands.

This book is sold with the understanding that neither the author nor the publisher is engaged in rendering legal, accounting, or other professional advice. If legal or other expert assistance is required, the services of a competent person should be sought.

Dedicated to
Lucille H. Delaware

Table of Contents

Publishers Note

Before proceeding, it is important to make a necessary disclaimer concerning legal advice. None of the information contained in this book is intended to constitute legal or other professional advice. You should not rely solely on the information contained in this book for making legal decisions. It is recommended one consult with an attorney or other professionals for specific advice tailored to your situation in the area of which you are doing business. The information contained herein has been obtained through sources deemed reliable but cannot be guaranteed as to its accuracy. Any information of special

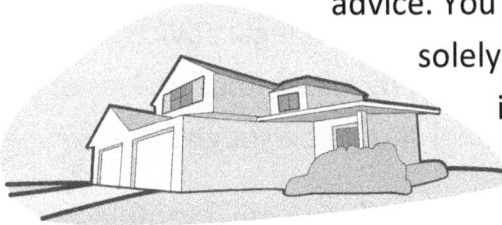

interest should be obtained through independent verification.

This publication is designed to provide information believed to be accurate based on research. It is designed to serve as guiding information in regard to the subject matter covered. One should conduct one's own independent inspection and investigation of the material presented as it relates to your area, as Real Estate laws and conditions are subject to change.

It is sold with the understanding that neither the author nor the publisher is engaged in rendering legal, accounting, investment, lending or any other professional advice. If legal advice or other expert assistance is required, the services of a competent professional should be sought.

All the names referred to in any example contained within this book are pseudonyms. Any perceived slight to any person or example related to or presented within this material is unintentional.

Introduction

The purpose of this book is to help those people that have been renting and have been struggling or have a challenging credit history to break free from this cycle and become home owners. In some cases, this may be their very first time buying a home. If this is the situation, then this could give you a golden ray of hope. In other scenarios, there may be people that were homeowners that lost their home, along with their good credit, and their hope of ever being a homeowner again. In this latter case, this book may represent a very real second chance.

Are you one of those half a million Americans that believe the prospect of becoming a homeowner is beyond your scope? Have you settled into a lifestyle of renting, merely because you see no way out? Or perhaps, you think there is no other way? Are you buried in credit problems, and the idea of navigating through the debris of the wreckage of your past mistakes on your financial picture better left in the graveyard of broken dreams?

There are a multitude of reasons to depart from this traditional part of the American Dream, and many may seem valid and true. If your Uncle George always told you that buying a home was next to impossible unless you were rich, and you always followed every advice uncle George gave you, then perhaps you should click this eBook closed!

Still reading? Well I'm glad you are still here. Would it surprise you to hear that you can become a homeowner, if you follow through and take 10 precise steps? It's true. Now the book title says they are 'Easy' and that is true. It does not mean they are short, just that they can be achieved. Time is an irrelevant concept with the purchase of real estate. It is better to be prepared, and do it right, to get the best possible deal for yourself, rather than rush it.

Some of the steps might be longer than others; it all depends on your given situation. However, each of the steps can be taken. If you patiently work your way through each step presented in this book, you will find you can navigate through each and every obstacle that is thrown at you in the process. The steps are not impossible, but may require some commitment and dedication on your part to complete them. This book is designed to be a simple guide to anyone venturing on this trail for the first time and serve as a road map.

It is also written with a focus on simplicity, to cover the basic steps to take to reach this goal. So if you are looking for comprehensive mortgage terms and tables, appraisal language and detailed property tax descriptions to put you to sleep, then you might be better off looking for another book. I have tried not to use complicated language within the basic text of this book, however, like any subject there are terms unique to the process. For that reason I have included a simple real estate glossary at the end of this book. With that, along with the magic of Kindle eBook dictionaries, this should be all you need should you find a term needs more clarity for you. One can also consult other real estate glossaries on the internet if further information is needed.

This book is not designed to replace the need for seeking professional advice from REALTORS®, Loan Officers, Mortgage Brokers, Appraisers, Home Inspectors, and any other number of professionals in the industry. In fact, it is quite the reverse! As an author, I encourage you to avail yourself of all of these professionals, as that is what they are there for, so use them every step of the way along your journey. This book is not intended to be a guide or advice to choosing a professional in any of these fields. The only advice I will offer on this is as follows: *Choose someone you enjoy working with.* More on that will be covered later.

This book follows a simple layout. The letters 'G-O-I-N-G-H-O-M-E' are the first letters of the first nine chapters, and cover the first nine steps. The last chapter you might call the 'exclamation point' (!) as it puts you in the 'driver's seat' as a homeowner, and gives you the steering wheel.

Use this book as a road map to the ultimate goal of becoming a homeowner and release yourself from forever paying rent. The 10 steps laid out in this text, if followed exactly, will help you arrive at your goal. If you skip any step, or skimp on any of them and find you have not gotten the end result of each step, the solution is very simple: Go back and complete the earlier missed step and continue, making sure all the others are complete, and you will get there. Failure to reach your goal is due to just one point; you missed or left incomplete an earlier step. If there is any general overall rule in this book, that is it.

Enjoy your journey!

Chapter One:

GETTING THE FEVER

Let's first examine the pros and cons of renting versus home ownership:

Mobility: Renting Vs Home Ownership

Renting offers one the ability to move without having to sell, which is probably the best overall benefit of renting. Usually the landlord will cover expenses such as lawn care and general maintenance that you would ordinarily have to cover as a homeowner. At least that is the appearance, as you are not writing checks for these items directly, but more often than not you are paying for these expenses imbedded into your rent.

It is a fact that all landlords are investors, and their investment is the house, multi-unit or apartment that you are renting. The return on their investment is your monthly rent, with which they cover all these expenses not to mention their profit. It is true that some investments are better than others, and some landlords lose money every month through poor management, but they still have the asset and may even write off any 'losses' on their taxes.

The downside to renting is that one pays every month only for the right to stay somewhere, but without the sense of permanency and limited control on what you can do to your 'space'. When one pays for rent, one is in fact buying an intangible and limited asset called 'time' or 'time to remain where one is' for a specified period defined in the lease, which is usually in 30 day increments. In other words, you are paying for the right to remain in that space with all your possessions for another 30 days of time. When that time expires, you must pay again, and the cycle repeats itself. If you do not pay, you eventually lose your right to remain there and must move, along with your possessions, elsewhere.

Another risk in renting is that one is relying on the landlord's maintenance of the place you are renting. If you sign a twelve month lease in March, and discover you do have working air conditioning in June, you would call the landlord. If he or she is not willing to fix or service it, you may be in for a very uncomfortable renting experience. If you have ever rented, you may have experienced something like this and that is why you are reading this book. There are also the other issues that come from renting, such as noisy neighbors, limited space for storage, and sometimes limited parking.

With homeownership, your monthly payments go towards paying for a tangible 'asset' which is your home. These monthly payments are in the form of a mortgage payment to a creditor. Up until 2007 in the U.S. residential real estate was appreciating in value on a steady trend, and one could project into the future the potential to be able to sell the home for more than you paid for.

This added value was called 'equity'. When the asset is appreciating in value in an improving market, one can sell the home and benefit from this increased equity. If you decided to move in 5 years, as long as you took care of the property, you can usually sell it for more than you originally paid in such a market. Even with the declining market values in the years on a national level since 2007, not every area of the country has suffered decline and some are recovering. The home values that present themselves in many markets now in 2013 represent great opportunities for new home buyers, as one can often get into a home that on a national average is as much as 30% less than what it was five years ago.

The downside to homeownership versus renting is that it can take longer to move because usually the home has to be sold first. It is not unreal for the transition of moving to take as much as four times longer than someone who seeks to rent. In some markets, finding the right buyer can take time. Additionally, as mentioned above, if you buy in a market that goes into decline during the time you live there, it can make it even more challenging to sell than under normal conditions.

Defaulting on Payment: Renting Vs Home Ownership

Now let's take a look at the comparison of what happens when someone stops paying rent, or in the case of home ownership, stops paying a mortgage. No one ever wants to do this, as it can be very bad for credit. However, it happens, so it is worth a comparison so one can merely see the differences.

In renting if one fails to pay their monthly rent, the risk is eviction. One may also risk losing one's possessions by having to abandon them, if eviction follows through and you have not worked out a new place to move to. Have you ever driven by an apartment complex or a house and witnessed the sight of a large pile of furniture, stereos, clothing and other personal possessions on the curb? This is a sadly commonplace negative associated with the displacement from eviction. Every State has a set of eviction laws, and they vary. The time can be longer in some places, and shorter in others. Ultimately, however, when time runs out you will have to leave.

If one does not pay a mortgage, one faces a process called foreclosure. In some types of financing, there is another process called forfeiture, which is similar to foreclosure and it has to do with what State you are living in, and what type of note you have on the home. If you are still unable to resolve the default, then eviction as described above will eventually follow once the foreclosure or forfeiture process runs out, as you lose your rights to the home. When one is evicted in renting, the landlord can pursue collections through the court for back rent and damages after you have left the premises. To collect any judgments they can report it on your credit report, or garnish your wages, etc.

With foreclosures there is no court process or garnishment after you leave, however, the report of a foreclosure can have an extreme negative impact on your credit. Foreclosures are their own category of default on a credit report, and have a greater negative impact than a judgment. So in comparison to renting versus owning a home and failing to pay, both can negatively impact your credit. It can take longer to be removed from the home in a foreclosure process in some States, but it is more damaging to your credit in the long run that a default in renting. A judgment from delinquent rent can always be settled at a later date and the negative impact reduced or removed, but a foreclosure cannot be removed so quickly. We will go more into this more in later chapters on credit.

A Financial Comparison

However, let's take another look at this comparison from a financial point of view. For the purpose of example, we will take two fictional characters named Andrew and Joy. Both have remained at similar sized homes for five years, in the same general area of town, with one exception, Andrew rents his home and Joy is a homeowner with a mortgage. Both homes are valued at around $120,000.00.

Andrew pays $900 a month rent, and Joy pays $900 a month on a mortgage payment, which includes her property taxes and insurance in the same payment.

In five years time, Andrew will have paid his landlord $54,000 in rent. He leaves the place in good shape, and the landlord refunds him a $900 security deposit which he paid 5 years earlier.

When he moves, he will be able to move within 30 days, but he will have no further funds coming to him. His contract with his landlord is over, and in the five years time his monthly rent has bought him time to stay there, and nothing more.

Joy will have paid the same $54,000 in the same time. Joy's $54,000 has gone to principle and interest payments on her 30 year mortgage. She originally bought the home for $110,000 and the current appraisal value is $125,000. She finds a buyer within 60 days, and accepts an offer for $122,000. In the five years her mortgage was paid down to $92,000. After closing fees, she receives at closing a check for approximately $25,000 on the sale of her home minus settlement fees.

So in comparison, Andrew's cost of living for 5 years for a residence was $54,000. Joy's cost of living for her residence was $54,000 minus $25,000 profit from her sale, equaling $29,000. Andrew paid $900 a month. Joy paid $483 a month, and walks away with enough money to put another down payment on another house wherever she wants to move to.

With this example, one can see there is a

benefit from home ownership over renting in a market with improving values. Still not convincing enough to get you in the fever of homeownership? Let's continue the story of Andrew and Joy.

Andrew has gotten a new job, and moves to another part of town and leases another house that is valued at $125,000, for a monthly rent of $950 a month. Joy, having been transferred to the same area of town buys a new home that is valued at $125,000. She puts $25,000 down and mortgages the remaining $100,000. Her monthly mortgage is $800 a month with property taxes and insurance, but she decides to make payments of $950 (paying an extra $150 a month on principle) to pay her loan down faster. Both Andrew and Joy remain in their individual residences another 5 years.

This time, Andrew has paid $57,000 for his residence, and when he moves he once again receives only his security deposit form his landlord. However, his security deposit has been reduced by $500 for damages to the carpet, so he is only returned $450 from the landlord.

Joy has paid the same $57,000 in mortgage payments in the same amount of time. Her home was appraised at $137,000 by recent appraisal. She finds a buyer within 60 days, and accepts an offer for $135,000. With her added efforts on the mortgage over the five years, she has paid an additional $9000 on her principle with her regular monthly payment, and her remaining balance on her loan is $75,000. After closing costs, she receives a check for $52,000 from the sale of her home.

By comparison now, Andrew has paid $950 a month for the past 5 years. Joy having paid $57,000 minus $52,000 she received from the sale of this home equals $5000. Take that $5000 and divide it by 60 months (5 years) and you will see that Joy's cost of living per month has been a mere $83.34 based on the same comparison.

This is a crude comparison, the numbers are rough, and it does not account for many other factors in the cost of living, much less all the various itemized expenses involved in selling real estate. Experts could argue that the numbers should be jockeyed around in different and more complicated ways, or that I haven't taken into account for declining home markets, rising property taxes, moving expenses, etc. Yes, those points can all be called valid. However, one cannot escape the comparison no matter how one adjusts the numbers: that Andrew's cost of living is not changing, and is in fact increasing with inflation, and Joy's cost of living is decreasing through continued long term homeownership. And that is the primary message of this comparison.

Then, there's freedom? Yes, freedom. When you rent, you have more restrictions on what you can do to a property because you are not the owner. When you own your home, you have the freedom to modify, change and improve your asset as you see fit in most cases. The only exception is if there is a home owners association or restrictive covenant that defines guidelines as to what can be done to the exterior of a home. Outside of this one exception, you are free to make the space your own, rather than adjusting to what is there.

Let's say you wanted to paint a room? As a homeowner, it's is just a journey to the hardware store for paint. As a renter, you have to seek permission from your landlord, abide by the terms of the leasing company, get approval on the colors and when all the work is completed you cannot take these improvements with you. As a homeowner you are the final decision maker on color, as a renter your lease might require you to seek approval from the property owner.

Many homeowners come to feel a sense of pride and caring for something they own. They tend to take better care of it too. Have you ever created something that was entirely your own? Can you recall that sensation of it being your creation? Homeownership can kindle that spirit in you, because you can create and build upon your investment through improvements and upgrades. It becomes more uniquely yours, the more you invest your energy into bettering the overall condition of your home.

In the above example with Andrew and Joy, let's say they both invested $5000 to improve their residence. Andrew's personally invested $5000 becomes the property of the landlord when he moves out, for good or bad. In Joy's case, it becomes the property of the new homeowner, and often will be paid for by the new homeowner through the increased value upon sale of the property. So as a homeowner, it's very easy to catch the fever of improving and preserving your investment. It begins to become a game, and you start to treat your residence as more than just a place to reside, but as a genuine asset: Real Estate that is yours.

In order to start on this trail to homeownership, you must first make a decision. That decision may have come to you already. If it has, then I hope that decision is 'I want to become a homeowner'. If it hasn't, then I would suggest you do the following: Go visit 5 people you know that rent, and 5 people you know that own their own homes. Draw up a list comparing rents and mortgage payments. Draw up another list comparing what you observe about their residence and living arrangements. Take both lists and compare for yourself whether renting or homeownership makes more sense to you after this.

If homeownership fever has started to get you, then let's move on...

Chapter Two:

ORGANIZING YOUR LIFE

Let's take a look at organizing your present income lines, and how you handle your finances to set you up for homeownership. The issues related to fixing credit problems will be covered in later chapters. First and foremost, we shall take a look at the subject of personal organization and 'organizing'.

Organizing is defined with such terms as 'structure' and 'order' as its key components. 'Structure' is defined as 'something composed of interrelated parts forming an organism or organization'. Just as your body is formed with organs such as a heart and kidneys, as 'interrelated parts' to continue surviving; your personal finances require parts for its 'organization'. 'Order' is defined as 'The sequence and arrangement of things'. So when we embrace the subject of 'organizing' personal finances, we are talking about having a sequence and arrangement of parts to form a complete whole called a 'financial system'.

When one is moving from the realm of renting to that of homeownership, it requires that a new organization occurs in ones habits, structure and order in the area of finances. To do so, one must work with a consistent and useable system that helps one stay organized at all times, as well as save money.

When you become a homeowner, you are in fact becoming an investor in 'Real Estate'. 'Real Estate' is defined as 'An asset of land, including buildings and improvements'. An 'Improvement' is defined as 'any structure built upon the land'. So to own 'Real Estate' we are talking about ownership of an asset. In financial terminology, an 'asset' increases in value, and a 'liability' decreases in value. It is generally considered that Real Estate increases in value, and is therefore an *asset*.

In this chapter, I will be covering two key areas that are the backbone of making that investment a smooth success. These two areas are *'a system for organizing your finances'* and *'establishing and following good credit behavior'*.

Now before you panic, and say 'Wait! My finances are a mess and I already know my credits in bad shape!'

Read on.

In the two chapters that follow this one I will address 'identifying credit problems', and 'neutralizing the negatives', giving you simple, foolproof tools to resolve these issues even before you go somewhere to apply for a loan.

So don't worry about what situation you are in currently. This system will help you keep order in before, during, and after you buy your home.

A SYSTEM FOR ORGANIZING YOUR FINANCES

The first most important action in organizing your finances is to find out exactly what the current scene is. Therefore, you must round up into one location all the bills and bill statements of anyone and everyone your owe money to.

A	B	C	D
Creditor	Total Amount Owed	Current Amount Due	Date Due
ABC Credit Card	$1234.55	$105.00	3 Dec 08
Ace Utility Co.	$85.00	$85.00	9 Dec 08
WFS Car Payment	$14,304	$304.00	15 Dec 08

Once you have done this, you want to make a list to put this all in order. Call it a 'bills summary' and break it down into four different columns on a sheet of paper; Column A: The Name of the creditor, Column B: The total amount owed, Column C: The amount of the current payment due, and Column D: The date the current payment is due. You will want to sort them in order of the date due, so that you can see the chronological use for this is an 'Excel®' spreadsheet. You can also do this with the home finance program Quicken® or any other variety of home finance software available. If you do not have a computer, then a simple lined paper, notebook or ledger will do. If you decide to do this in a ledger, get one with six columns. They can easily be acquired from any office supply store. The two extra columns can be used for indicating the date a bill was paid, and any other notes you care to write in the last column to help you keep a running record of your finances.

I once helped an associate do this simple action, and he was so amazed how his world suddenly stopped resembling a merry-go-round. He could see for the first time on paper his monthly expenses, and see where his money was going. He was then able to economize in areas, and see the results in a short amount of time. Within three months, he had gone from having no reserves, to building up enough savings to place a down payment on a house. So this basic organization step is not to be underestimated in importance, just because it sounds so simple.

Taking this one step further, now that you can see where you are and what your situation is, you might have come to the conclusion that you need to change some things. The fact is that is the truest realization you could ever come to.

Realize that if you are renting and you have poor credit, then you may have a personal situation that you need to confront. This may require that you change the way you have been spending up to now. You have to embrace this idea, or you will never be able to put any kind of working structure into your life.

I had a friend named Luke once that I sat down to do this exercise. He had been having trouble paying his bills on time, and frequently found himself paying extra service fees and charges due to his own neglect. Together we collected all his bills from all over his apartment, (and there were many). We spent a few hours on a Saturday afternoon putting them in order on a spreadsheet. Throughout the process of putting this together, Luke was squirming in his chair and making noises of frustration. However, we managed to reach the bottom of the pile, and he discovered for the first time he was able to see what his bills summary actually looked like. From there he was able put together a list of his monthly income, and made a comparison of the two. After that he was able to put together a monthly plan to control his own expenditures, and eliminate expenses he that he deemed to be impractical. This simple action placed a great deal of order into his personal finances, and he saw the immediate value of keeping this summary current from there on out.

A few months after putting in and keeping in his bills summary, Luke reported to me that he was not feeling so 'hectic' about his bills anymore, and that he had developed some games for himself to pay off a few credit cards and his car loan by the end of the quarter, and he was ahead of his target on it.

So what are some of the basic things you can do to reduce your bills, once you have your bills summary organized? Take each bill individually, and run it down the following list:

- Is this a necessary expenditure?

- Does some other provider or creditor offer the same or similar service for less?

- Can I eliminate this expenditure?

- Can I consolidate this bill or expenditure and save money?

- Can I share or split the cost of this expenditure with someone else, and reduce my liability?

Now, with your bills summary in hand, let's look at the financial picture before you. Reduce or eliminate what you can by following the above list on every bill. Examine your gross earnings versus your expenditures. Is the picture in any way in need of improvement? As we move away from this organization step, 'how you bank your money' then becomes the next crucial step.

ACQUIRING A GOOD, WORKABLE SYSTEM OF MONEY MANAGEMENT

A common system found in many families I have observed is as follows: Money wages or salaries are banked each week. That is, it's all deposited into one checking account, which both husband and wife are signatories of, and both write checks from the account until it is depleted and then the cycle is repeated.

Does this sound familiar? Have you or someone you known ever followed this system? Have you experienced or seen others experience the inability to pay bills, or fall short of funds in some manner each week? Perhaps they experience this at the end of the month, because they are using this same system?

MALCOLM'S SYSTEM

Earn Money, Spend Money, Borrow Money

I had a good friend named Malcolm that I knew many years ago. He had a tool repair business that he worked very hard at. Each Friday he would take home his earnings, and by Monday morning he would not have money for breakfast.

Over the weekend he would find every way he could think of to spend his money. Sometimes he paid his bills, but mostly he operated off of an "impulse buying" mentality, where he would walk into a 'bait and tackle shop' (because Malcolm loved to fish) and spend $50.

He would then stop at a convenience store and spend $20 there, and so forth, and so on, until he ran out of cash. On Monday's he would borrow money from me, and on Friday he would pay me back, and the cycle would repeat itself. That was Malcolm's way of handling his finances. He had no system, and as a result he was never able to rise above leasing a mobile home in the country.

Malcolm's system of finances doesn't seem to buy him any long term future. In Malcolm's case, whenever he had an emergency in life where he needed a large amount of money to resolve it, he had no reserves. His only recourse was to borrow the money from family members or friends and fall further into debt. Despite the brief moments of happiness from the new items he had purchased, he was miserable and unhappy because each year he would sink further and further into debt.

MR. GRAY'S SYSTEM

As another case example, I knew an older gentleman once (whom I will call Mr. Gray) who showed me a system he used to manage his funds. I thought it to be a sensible and simple system which deserved consideration and review.

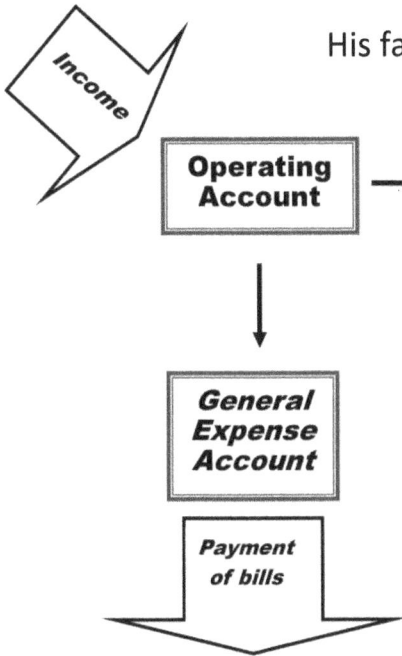

His family had three accounts.

Income

Operating Account → Reserve Account

General Expense Account

Payment of bills

All the weekly funds were deposited into one account called the 'Operating Account' or call it Account #1. Into the Operating Account, he only made deposits, and never wrote any expense checks.

Mr. Gray then had a second account. The second account he called his 'General Expense' account or Account #2. To this account he would transfer from the 'Operating Account' (#1) the exact amount of the bills and expenses due that week only. He would get the exact amount of the transfer from his summary of bills, which he kept up religiously every week. This account has a small extra amount that he never spent in it that he called his 'float'. This extra money gave him the ability to write checks from the account while deposits were clearing without running the risk of bouncing checks.

He then had a third account (#3) which he called his 'Reserve/Investment' account. Each week he would transfer 5% to 25% of his gross earnings to this account. He would never withdraw money from these funds, except when he was moving it to an investment such as a bond or mutual fund. I asked him once how he decided how much to set aside each week in this account. He responded by telling me that when he began this system, he started with a small amount, and then each week he would challenge himself to spend less money that week than the week before in some way. Sometimes, he would skip the trip to the café for lunch and brown bag a lunch that day. Other days he would walk to work, instead of taking a cab. That extra money he saved, he would transfer in addition to his next weeks' transfer, and it grew from there.

Every week he would play a game with

himself to save a little more, and soon he became very efficient at it. There were weeks where he put the same amount in each week, and then there were others where he managed to put a little more. He stressed to me that this third account should be the highest interest bearing saving account or 'money market' you can find, and move the money monthly or quarterly as it builds to larger more secure investments. He also highly recommended an 'Individual Retirement Account' or 'IRA' as a third or fourth account.

In later years he told me he turned his 'operating account' into a savings account, to further restrict his own temptation of writing checks from it and also to have the account earn interest. From this account he would make a weekly transfer of funds to other accounts only. He would hold sums needed for payments of larger bills, such as his mortgage, until he needed to transfer it.

Now in Mr. Gray's case, he had very few overdue bills, as he had been using his system for 20 years when I met him. He was able to concentrate on building his reserves, more and more as time went on.

He did tell me that in the early years, when he had backlogged his bills, he would meet the immediate obligations first, then set 3 to 5% into reserves, and put the rest into paying his bills down. In this way he was able to economize on his spending habits, increase his income, pay off his back debt, and at the same time created a reserve for the future.

It is important to note that Mr. Gray's system did not involve the use of modern day 'debit cards'. Use of debit cards can sabotage this type of system, as all too often the transactions do not get all recorded and it can throw your personal accounting off.

Over the years I have recommended to friends Mr. Gray's simple system, and have seen very great results from it when applied. I have used this system myself, and have come to realize it is a great way to control your expenses and it actually made it fun to earn more money.

Now when you look at this system, you might say 'Wait! That doesn't give me enough to live on each week for general expenses!' Well, that's where you have to take a hard cold look at what you are spending your money on, and how much money you are actually earning.

You may have to cut back with hard decisions on expenses, or get additional sources of income established or both to make this system work. However, if you examine it closely, all the bills would still get paid. It does force in a savings, and it also regulates the amount you spend. It acts as a preventative for over-spending, and will give you tools to get your bills summary reduced. As an additional note, it places ones attention not on spending money so it goes to zero, but instead one begins to direct ones attention onto earning more money so as not to disrupt the stability.

You may have observed that if there is a large sum of money in one account, it is easy to spend, and it seems to disappear fast. It is so easy to go out and buy a motorcycle! After all, it is summer! Not that there is anything wrong with buying a motorcycle or even a new car, but if your aim is owning a home, and getting rid of an already existing debt, then it may not be a sensible purchase.

In using Mr. Gray's system, the same amount of money divided between three or more accounts, looks a lot smaller. Amazingly, it doesn't seem to disappear as fast. This is especially true if you limit the uses for each account. It allows you to build reserves and control spending.

PAULINE'S SYSTEM

Let's explore some other systems of financial management. I once knew a lady named Pauline that showed me her system for managing her finances. Pauline's system was similar in nature to Mr. Gray's, but much more involved. Her formula was to deposit all her funds into a general expense account. From this account, she would set aside funds into bonds and Certificates of Deposit (CD's) weekly or monthly.

These bonds and CD's would mature at various intervals of 3, 6, 9 and 12 months or longer at her discretion. She would make this decision on time based on the size of the deposit. As the bonds and CD's cycled around and matured, she would remove the interest and re-invest the principle into another similar investment.

This gave her a residual income from her maturing investments, and it worked quite well for her. It did require a steady accumulation of investments into these bonds and CD's, as they usually did not produce a tremendously high

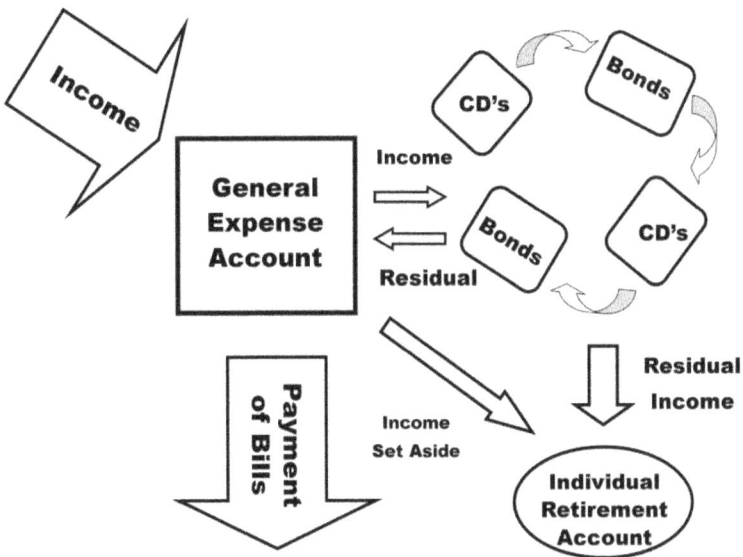

interest rate, however, the quantity she continually invested allowed for a modest and steady residual income for herself as she grew older.

She would pay her bills from her general expense account, and as the years went by she was also able to pay some from her residual income from these investments. She later transferred the residual income to an IRA and other retirement accounts where she further invested her returns. Now this was at a time in history where interests rates were higher, so it was possible to do this as her reserves grew.

DONOVAN'S SYSTEM

Another system I came across was used by a man I knew named Donovan. Donovan had a small business, and he also had a part time job at a factory. Each week he would deposit his funds into an 'Operating Expense Account' and from there distribute his funds to his business creditors, his IRA, his personal account and his income tax set aside account. From his income tax set aside account he would invest these funds in short term Bonds and CD's as Pauline did, while the money was sitting around waiting to pay the IRS. He explained to me that by keeping his tax set asides in bonds and CD's, it removed the temptation he had for borrowing from those funds. As a result, he just concentrated on making more money whenever he needed more, rather than tap into his reserves or IRA.

From his personal account, he would pay his

personal bills. Once again, pointing out to me that by carefully distributing his money each week, he learned that he needed to make more money if he wanted to achieve his goals.

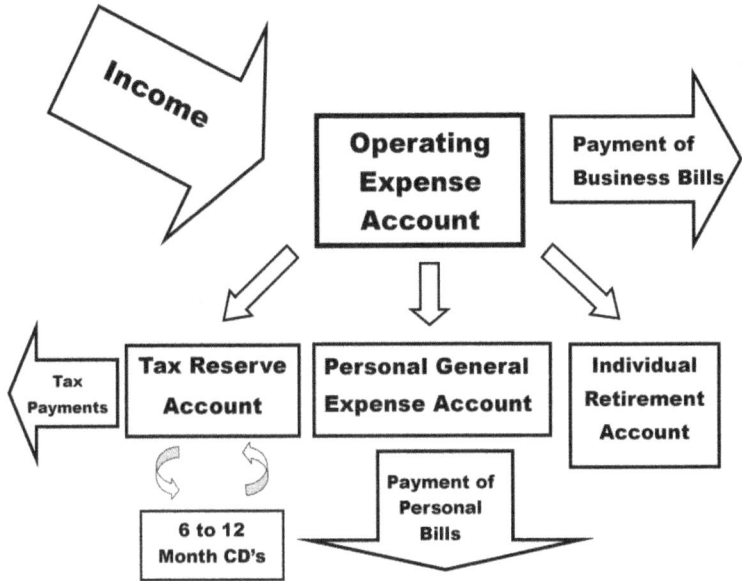

So this is where you have to make a decision to change your way of doing things. Adopt a new system that does not create a dangerous situation on your finances each month. Doing so will greatly improve your outlook on life.

When you are seeking to buy a home, it is often in your best interest to have some money to put down as a down payment. There are many programs that offer 100% financing, but they can also charge higher interest rates and cost you a lot more in the long run. With changes in the National Mortgage market since early 2007, many of the 100% financing programs are disappearing. So a better strategy is to plan and prepare for placing a down-payment on your new home, if at all possible.

In either case, it helps to strengthen your loan application if you have reserves, whether or not you use them. Thus is best to get in a system on your weekly and monthly expenditures that controls and regulates the direction or flow of money. If you can keep a good control, and regulate where it goes, you will soon find money starts to work for you.

The origin of the word 'Currency' comes from the root word 'Current', as in: *'A current in a river'*. If you think of money in terms of a river, then it is easy to think in terms of flows. Just as you can control the flow of water in a river, and pool it up to form a lake, so you can do the same with money if you establish a system that gets this result. A very good book to read to open doors for you on creating more income is 'Multiple Streams of

Income' by Robert G. Allen. This book will give you great information on how to increase your income streams.

Mr. Gray's system I have found to be quite useful. There are perhaps many accountants that could recommend a more expanded system, and by all means, use these if they work for you.

This brings us to the question 'What is the best system?'

The best answer I can give you is: *The one that works for you.*

However, keep in mind this system must help you control the flow of your money, pay your bills and build reserves to be ideal for reaching the goal of homeownership. Keep these points in mind when establishing your system:

- Control the flow of money

- Pay your bills

- Build reserves

- Keep to your goal of homeownership

It is important to note that you should pay your bills as a priority over building reserves; however you should never forget to pay yourself. By 'pay yourself' I do not mean to go shopping for new clothes, but more exactly to pay yourself by building a reserve for tomorrow.

A book that gives great insight into systems such as this is '*The Millionaire Next Door*' by Thomas Stanley and William Danko. This book emphasizes the importance of building solid reserves, and is based on a comprehensive study of millionaires across America.

MAINTAINING YOUR RECORDS

Another key element of organization, is keeping an efficient record system for your accounts. I recommend keeping at the very least a filing system with a file for each creditor or billing agency you have. Utilization of computer programs like Microsoft Money® and Quicken® can also go a long way to keeping you organized. If you don't have a computer, then use ledgers and keep separate sections for each of your accounts, as well as your bills.

It is also important to keep records of bills paid, even of accounts you have closed. You may never know when you will have use for those records, and you will find out more about the importance of this as you read later chapters.

How long should you keep records? I recommend at least 5 years. The reason for this will become clearer in the next few chapters if you have to work on cleaning up credit reports. Records can be a pain to keep, particularly old records. I recommend keeping a two to four drawer metal filing cabinet, and then transferring the contents to banker boxes every 1-2 years.

Valuable documents that are irreplaceable or hard to replace such as deeds, titles, birth certificates, stocks, bonds, life insurance policies, wills, etc. should be kept in a fire-proof safe or safety deposit box at a bank as a common sense measure. This should be done for any record or items you may need in the future, and could not risk losing to a fire, water damage, natural disaster, robbery or general neglect.

When it comes to organizing your life, the time invested in a little basic up front organization can save you many, many hours of headache in the years to come. So set up an area of your living space for your personal administration, be it a desk, office or closet. Set up a system of organization. Make sure it includes a structure for keeping records, and carries a sense of order throughout.

What is the best system for maintaining records? One that you will use, and can find records when you need them, without delay.

Easy access to records, and keeping good order in their sorting, is the best way to start on the road to a foundation of good credit.

ESTABLISHING A FOUNDATION OF 'GOOD CREDIT'

What is good credit? Where did this 'credit' thing start? One can perhaps envision a time in the olden days when there were farming communities, and being that most of the people in the community relied on their annual harvest to cover their expenses, they would sometimes fall short on funds in between harvests. Systems of loaning money during these times were developed, and by providing this service, the farmers agreed to pay back these loans plus interest.

One could perhaps continue this story into the future, and see how times changed and more and more this concept of extending credit expanded to other industries. Until we have the system in present time of credit being extended as easily as swiping a plastic card through a machine. The interest payments are worked into a convenient billing system that takes forever (it seems) to pay off the original debt. The ease of borrowing and spending has created situations for some people where they have more bills due than they have earnings, and so fall behind. This is called "delinquency" in the eyes of people that loan money. If one misses a payment, or neglects the debt entirely, it is flagged as a "bad mark" on a credit history.

In the world of 'mortgage financing' exists the concept of 'good credit' versus 'bad credit'. In order to understand this section, let's examine what is meant by good credit and bad credit.

Over the years lenders of money have tried to establish criteria of what defines a good credit history, and what defines a bad one. Many systems were tried over the years. In the 1970's and 1980's comprehensive and extensive loan applications were taken, which took weeks of pulling records. The person seeking the loan had to provide these, before a decision was ultimately made by usually a committee as to whether or not the loan would be granted. In seeking to create a better system, a company called 'Fair, Isaac & Company' developed a scoring system for various types of credit behavior. Their idea was to take someone's reported credit history, assign a numerical value to every aspect of the report, good or bad, and arrive at a single number.

This single number was ultimately called a 'FICO' score, having been developed by Fair, Isaac & Co. (F.I.CO). Credit scoring became a method of determining the likelihood that credit users will pay back the creditors. It soon grew into the universal measuring stick for all credit histories.

FICO began its pioneering work with credit scoring in the late 1950s and, since then, their 'scoring' system has become widely accepted by lenders as a reliable means of credit evaluation. A credit score attempts to condense a borrowers' credit history into a single number.

There later came into being three separate credit evaluation companies that used the FICO scoring system, and banks from all over the country began to use the one closest to them in their region. These three companies' names are: *Experian*, *Equifax* and *TransUnion*. They are often referred to as the 'Credit Bureaus' or the 'Bureaus'.

Originally, lenders would only send information to the one bureau that was closest to them geographically. It was possible in those days to have a poor credit history with one bureau, and move to another part of the country and find you had a clean credit history. With the advent of technology such as computers and the internet, those days soon passed quickly. Now it is not uncommon for a creditor reporting a poor credit performance to report the information to two, or all three bureaus. In fact, it is common practice.

Today these three companies are regulated by an arm of the U.S. Government called the 'Federal Trade Commission' which oversees fairness in the execution of lending practices in the country. Fair, Isaac & Co. and the credit bureaus do not reveal how credit scores are computed. Very few people know all the formulas. The Federal Trade Commission after extensive review has ruled this to be acceptable. However, through observation and comparison of many different credit reports, some of this information has been uncovered by a sort of 'reverse-engineering' approach to a study of credit scores. Therefore, there is a lot of information available from experts on at least the major things that impact a credit score.

FICO SCORING AND YOU

So what does a FICO score have to do with you? Well, believe it or not, you have a FICO score calculated on you based on information reported to three separate credit bureaus. These organizations which are called Credit Bureaus, and they are once again: *Experian, TransUnion* and *Equifax*. Each of these bureaus uses the FICO scoring system, and calculates a single number that is your credit score.

These Bureaus receive their information from creditors with whom you had accounts, as well as collection agencies, government organizations, etc. Each of the three Credit Bureaus will often have a different number calculated on you identifying your credit score, depending on which creditor reported to which bureau. Some creditors report to all three, others report only to one or two. So the credit scores can vary between the three bureaus, despite their use of the same scoring model.

To determine your credit score, credit bureaus analyze an individual's credit history. They also look at your credit mix, new credit, your payment history and how much you owe. They examine these and many other factors, including some of the following:

➢ Any history of late payments you might have.

➢ The amount of time credit has been established.

➢ The amount of credit versus the amount of credit you have available.

➢ The length of time you have resided at your present residence.

➢ Negative credit information, such as bankruptcies, charge offs, collections, etc.

➢ Types of accounts you as a borrower have: Mortgages, car loans, credit cards, etc.

➢ Any records of closed accounts by any
creditor that chooses to report it.

There are as many as 40 different factors that
are reviewed when a persons' credit history is
analyzed, and only FICO knows all the criteria. The
credit bureaus keep the exact formulas a closely
guarded secret, so there can be many factors that
affect a credit score that go well beyond the scope
of this book.

The credit score is based on this *secret
formula* that identifies the degree of your credit risk
to a lender.

So what is a 'risk'? Someone that is
considered a credit risk is deemed to be anyone
that by review of credit history and past
performance is likely to default on future payments.
The past is used to predict the future when it comes
to credit reports.

The credit score is the number used as a
benchmark to identify the level of credit risk a
person is. More on credit score numbers will be
discussed in Chapter 4, but for now, let's look at
what areas of a person's credit history are factored

into the scoring process.

THE 'BORROWER' DEFINED

A 'Borrower' is considered to be anyone that borrows money from a lending source. The moment you open a credit card, for example, you are considered a 'Borrower'. In all credit report reviews, you will see reference to you as a *borrower*. Your creditors report to credit bureaus on your history as a borrower with their company. From here on in this text you will see the term *borrower* used quite often when referring to credit reports and scores.

I will go into more on understanding, and resolving credit problems in later chapters. It is important to understand at this point that having a system of organizing is essential to being able to sort out any prior lack of organization. Credit reports are a reflection on how organized you were in the payment and performance on your obligations, and so therefore it becomes a major step to sort out on the road to home ownership.

Chapter Three:

IDENTIFYING CREDIT PROBLEMS

A creditor reviewing someone's credit history will place that borrower somewhere on a scale with an 'Ideal Credit Risk' at the top to a 'High Credit Risk' at the bottom. The 'Ideal Credit Risk' would be a person that one could extend money to, and be certain and confident that the borrower would pay it back per the terms agreed.

A 'High Credit Risk' one would not be inclined to extend credit to, as there is more than a very high probability that you will never see your money again. Someone in the middle might be considered a 'marginal' credit risk. This criterion is based solely on a borrower's credit history, and can mean the difference between a detailed and involved loan application process, and a short one. With this one can see that credit history plays a crucial role in determining the potential risk to a lender.

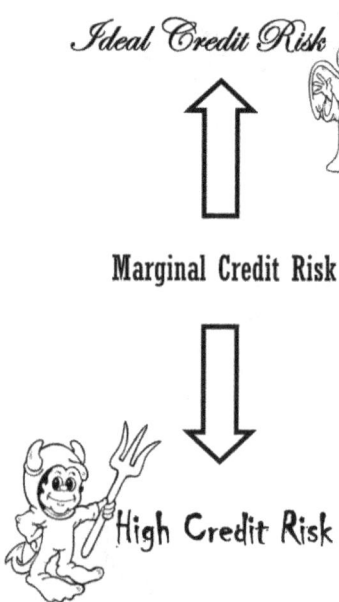

Ideal Credit Risk

Marginal Credit Risk

High Credit Risk

One falling along this scale in the middle is generally considered a 'Marginal' risk. So ultimately, your credit score value determines where an individual falls on this scale. The higher the value, the lower the lender of money perceives a credit risk. The lower the value, the higher one is considered a risk. However, these values can change over one's lifetime.

One can go through a period of rough finances, and have a lower score. One can also go through a period of their life where things improve, and if one does not go back and correct the past, despite your new improved credit in other areas, you can simply rise to be only a 'marginal' credit risk.

Whereas if you really are dedicated to changing your operating basis, and going back to correct the negatives, you can raise your score to the highest value possible.

As the actual credit scoring process is only known to a select few, it is difficult to be precise in giving complete credit advice.

This text is not intended to represent a complete picture on all the elements considered in the scoring process. Despite this, over the years, experts in lending have been able to isolate key areas that have proven time and again to improve one's overall credit score.

The following are some key areas to understand when trying to establish good credit behavior:

PAYMENT HISTORY

A historic review of how payments have been made in the past is considered to be a borrowers 'payment history' as reported by creditors to the credit bureaus.

They are roughly categorized as follows:

➢ A borrower who has never had a late payment on their history is the profile of the ideal risk.

➢ A borrower that has had isolated late payments displays the ability to recover from possibly difficult situations by taking responsibility for their obligations and bringing them current and keeping them current for an extended period of time.

➢ Borrowers who are consistently late in paying creditors reveal a general disregard for their payment responsibilities, and are considered a non-optimum credit risk.

➢ A borrower with no credit history can be regarded as an unknown, and therefore erroneously categorized as a potential risk, despite evidence of negative items. The lack of credit history creates a 'void of information' as the potential borrower has no performance record either way of demonstrating 'responsibility' or 'lack of responsibility' with a line of credit.

OPEN ACCOUNTS

The ideal borrower will have several open accounts. An open account is any line of credit you currently have with any lender, whether or not any money is owed on the account. This could be a credit card, car loan or mortgage.

The account is considered to be 'open' as long as neither the borrower nor the lender has asked for the account to be closed. The use of credit in the past will prove the borrower understands these obligations.

The fact that other creditors have extended credit indicates the consumer has already met some type of lending standard. A borrower with no accounts open will receive a lower score on this area as opposed to a borrower with several open accounts.

TYPES OF ACCOUNTS

Mortgages: Because of the amount of debt, a real estate mortgage is treated as a most serious financial obligation. A consumer who has been granted a mortgage in the past is the best risk because they have already displayed the ability to manage this type of financial responsibility. Per their own text, the lenders generally view an individual who has only rented or lived with family members poses a much higher risk because the only consequence to not paying rent was finding a new residence.

➢ Installment loans: Installment loans are weighted as the second most important financial obligation. Installment loans such as ones on automobiles, boats and other equipment show the ability to make a fixed payment for a predetermined period of time.

➢ Revolving Credit: Finally, the use of revolving credit such as credit cards is used in determining credit scoring. Since revolving credit allows the consumer to use up to the credit limit repeatedly, these debts have no end date. Because minimum payments are so low and the principle is usually not reduced by minimum payments, revolving credit is given the least weight in determining credit risk of the three listed here.

LENGTH OF CREDIT HISTORY

The length of credit history in very important in determining the credit score. A consumer who has used credit for many years paints a picture of what the future may hold. For example, the consumer who has used credit for 30 years most likely has experienced several economic recessions and therefore should have the ability to handle future economic difficulties.

The reverse of this example is the consumer who has had credit for only two years and may not have experienced economic turmoil. A short credit history cannot predict future performance accurately.

PUBLIC RECORDS

Public records include items such as liens, judgments, foreclosures and bankruptcies. These items weigh heavily in credit scoring. Public records display the historical need for a creditors' use of the court systems in an attempt to reclaim unpaid debts. The need for previous creditors to resort to legal action in order to be repaid represents high or 'bad' risk for the new creditors.

COLLECTIONS & 'CHARGE-OFFS'

Collections and 'charge-offs' include items for which payments ceased to be made, and were therefore turned over to a collection agency, or written off as bad debts. A creditor will report such an account condition to the credit bureau, and it will be marked as such on the credit history.

ACCOUNT BALANCES

The balance on accounts plays an important role in determining credit scores. Account balances on mortgage and installment loans show the time that has passed since opening the accounts.

These balances also demonstrate whether the debt is being managed responsibly by showing the amount of time that has passed since a late payment has been made.

In the case of revolving credit accounts, the

balances show how the consumer uses credit. The ideal balance on revolving debt seems to be 30% of the available credit limit. Remember the exact FICO formula is a secret, so this is just an estimate. However, the 30% figure has proven to be ideal because it creates history, which can be reported, yet it shows restraint on the part of the consumer.

10 TIPS TO INCREASE A CREDIT SCORE

You might ask, how can I increase my score?

A credit score is largely based upon past performance patterns on a borrowers handling of debt. This past history is used by lenders to predict the future. When a person demonstrates a pattern, this pattern more or less is deemed to be expected to continue in the future.

When a creditor views a poor performance record by a borrower on a credit report, they will consider the pattern is likely to continue, and therefore decline to extend credit. Therefore establishing good credit patterns today can improve the way your credit report appears in the future.

While it is difficult to increase your score over

the short run, here are some 10 tips to help increase your score over a period of time. (Please remember that the exact formula for credit scoring is not known in full, so the following list is just good common sense advice passed along to me by experts in the industry that they have been able to determine improves credit scores. Apply whatever makes sense to you.

Pay your bills on time. Late payments and collections can have a serious impact on your score.

Do not apply for credit frequently. Having a large number of inquiries on your credit report can worsen your score. Inquiries to your credit report occur whenever you authorize someone to pull your report (applying for a new credit card, loan, etc.) If too many inquiries show up on an account in a short period of time, this can be a red flag. Inquiries stay on your credit report for 12 months. For example, if you intended to add four new credit cards, you would be better off applying for two every 6 months, rather than 4 at once.

Reduce your credit-card balances. If you are "maxed" out on your credit cards, or over your credit limit, this will affect your credit score negatively. Get them paid down. It will also save you money on penalties and over-limit fees.

If you have limited credit, obtain some or get additional credit if you don't have enough to demonstrate a 'credit history'. Credit applications for new credit cards can be found at most major department stores and even some gas stations.

If you have no major credit cards, this is a simple and easy way to establish some accounts. Not having sufficient credit can negatively impact your score. This can be as simple as opening a credit card that you only use for small purchases and pay the balance off each month.

Do not close long term accounts. Too many times borrowers get into a game of 'get rid of all the credit cards' and close long term existing accounts. This can have a negative impact on your score. You are better off to leave them open and not use them, rather than close them.

Each account on a credit report is marked with a date indicating when the account was originally opened. If you close a long term account, this will greatly shorten your 'length of credit history' and reduce your score. I had a friend years ago named Carol that had her own unique method to keep herself restrained from using her own credit cards. She would freeze them in a block of ice in her freezer. She claimed that she would have to work too hard at it in order to use them, and would change her mind on that impulse purchase to avoid the trouble.

Reduce your credit-card balances to 1/3 of the credit limit on each card, and if you need additional credit add more cards rather than charge up them up to the limit.

This will keep your payments low, but also demonstrate restraint on your credit report. If you have high balances, transferring part of the balances to new or other cards to below the 1/3 level can improve your scores. Also paying them down to below the 1/3 level will accomplish the same results.

Do not make just the minimum payment when paying for credit cards. If you at least make each payment a little more than what the minimum is; it will be a better reflection on your credit score. Whenever possible, double the payments to help reduce balances faster.

Debt-to-available-credit ratio: The amount of money a person has in outstanding debt, compared to the amount of credit available on all of the individual's credit cards and credit lines. The higher a person's debt to available credit, the more risky the individual appears to potential lenders.

Stay with an employer for over 2 years before applying for a major loan. A frequent change of employers in less than a two year time frame creates an unstable employment picture for the lender. If you must make a job change, stay within the same occupation. For example, don't switch from being in an accounting position to suddenly becoming a full time hair-dresser, unless you can prove a prior long term successful employment history in that capacity.

If you are accustomed to moving every six months, you might consider changing your habits on this. According to loan officers reviewing credit applications, frequent moving within a two year period prior to a loan creates an unstable picture for the underwriter of the loan. One who moves too frequently (such as 4 to 6 times in a two year period) is likely to be hard to find should the account become delinquent. If can stay at one residence for at least two years before applying for a loan, this is ideal. However, one can at least keep this point in mind and minimize the number of moves they make. This will help to create a stable image in the eyes of the underwriter.

The importance and significance of credit reports and credit scores have increased dramatically in the loan approval process, as well as determining interest rates. The report will show how individuals, couples or partnerships have handled past debts and various credit accounts. So establishing these good credit habits can go a long way when contemplating becoming a homeowner.

It is also important to realize when reviewing the above list that not everyone will be able to get all the points in, but one can strive to get a majority of them in good condition before sitting down with a loan officer.

OBTAINING YOUR CREDIT INFORMATION FOR FREE

Now that you have a better idea on how to

organize your life to avoid credit problems, let's take a look at your rights as a consumer and how to identify credit problems.

The first thing that you will want to do is to find out if there are any potentially negative items being reported on your credit reports. You can obtain a free copy of your credit reports by mail from each of the three credit bureaus (Experian, TransUnion and Equifax) or by logging onto the following website: *www.annualcreditreport.com*

You are entitled to one free copy of your credit report per year from each of these three bureaus. These reports will not include your credit score. You can request your report more often; however, you will be required to pay a fee for this service. Please note, you can get your credit score at this site, but they charge an additional fee for this service.

A good strategy with working with this website is to pull one of the three credit bureaus every four months. That way you can access all three within the full year cycle, but have a good personal picture of your credit reports three times a year. Certainly not all information will be the same on each report, as explained earlier, but if you are going to apply the strategies for repairing a credit report as will be discussed later, this will work quite well.

Important Note: Whenever you access your credit report online at any of the three credit bureaus, you will be required to set up a log-on name and password. I recommend making a written record of this information, and storing it in a secure place. Entering the wrong password later can result in you being locked out for several months.

Additionally you can visit the following website and pay approximately $40 to have all three reports pulled with scores at once: *www.myfico.com*

You can also write to the three credit bureaus and request your reports. When writing to these companies to get a credit score, they require full name, addresses for the past 5 to 6 years, Social Security number, birth date, home phone number and signature.

You should call beforehand to find the exact

cost of getting a credit score.

The credit bureau addresses and phone numbers are:

Equifax
P.O. Box 740241
Atlanta, GA 30374
Phone: 1-800-685-1111

Experian
P.O. Box 2002
Allen, TX 75013
Phone: 1-888-397-3742

TransUnion
P.O. Box 1000
Chester, PA 19022
Phone: 1-800-888-4213

Once you have the report in hand, either from obtaining it online or receiving it in the mail, you will need to examine it for negative items. The main items that will pull a score down dramatically will be listed in a section entitled *'potentially negative items'* or sometimes *'derogatory items'*.

These can include the following: *delinquent accounts, collection accounts, public records, charge offs, vehicle repossessions, foreclosures* and *bankruptcy accounts.* These will be summarized in the report with notations of the date it was reported and recorded. The names and addresses of creditors and organizations reporting will also be printed on the report.

When you obtain a copy of your credit report, you will want to read through all the information and verify if it is accurate. By taking steps to pull your own reports, you can take a lot of the mystery out of the lending process. Obtaining copies of your own report does not have a negative impact on your score. You are entitled to this information in accordance with the *Fair Credit Reporting Act*, which we will go into in the next chapter.

Be wary of other companies that charge you a monthly fee for the service of monitoring your credit report, however, as many of them pull your credit scores and reports so often this creates continuous 'inquiry' into your credit report and this can bring your score down as well.

In the long run it is better to do it yourself, every four months on *www.annualcreditreport.com*

and pull a different bureau, than to have one of these services tap your report monthly.

WHAT ABOUT A ZERO CREDIT SCORE?

What if you look at you credit score and discover that it is a zero or 'no score'? What do you do in that regard? Essentially a zero score is not a negative, but it is not considered desirable either. It means you have no reported credit history.

Sure, you may have bills you pay to utility companies, landlords, cell phones, etc. However these types of bills do not report to a credit bureau. Therefore, even if your performance on these has been impeccable, they do not impact what is reported on your credit bureau.

The main types of credit lines that report on a credit bureau that is positive when paid on time fall into three categories:

- Mortgages

- Fixed Lines of credit (Like a car loan for example)

- Revolving lines of credit

Usually one cannot get a mortgage unless one has either a fixed line or revolving line of credit history. To build up a score from zero, the easiest way to start is with a revolving line of credit such as a credit card. Sometimes it can take a few months for one of these to start reporting on your credit report. In that case, one will want to consult with a lender who is perhaps more familiar with credit cards that you can apply for that might report within 30 days instead of 60 or 90 days.

Once a revolving line of credit is opened, the best course of action is to make 1 or 2 small purchases a month on them, and then pay them off in full at the end of the month for approximately 3-4 months in a row to get the good reporting history to start to build. This will have a positive impact on your score. You may also want to have more than one open, so that it is not the only thing showing on your credit report.

What is most important to understand about credit reports is that it is not just the score that one has, but also the history. Having only one credit card showing on a credit report may be a reason you are denied a mortgage too. It is not just the score that is important, but the number of different lines of credit being reported as 'pays as agreed' on the report. Their length of history on the report will also impact the score. The longer they are on the report being paid as agreed, the better.

Sometimes building a history from a zero score can take as much as twelve months for it to be good enough to apply and get approved for a mortgage.

Ones best action would be to open 2 or 3 credit cards, and charge a tank of gas or some groceries on them each month, and make the payments on time without fail.

Pay off the balance each month, and then let one of the cards carry a balance for a month or so, then pay it off. What you are trying to demonstrate on your credit history is a responsible credit pattern of behavior.

Chapter Four:

NEUTRALIZING THE NEGATIVES

As gone over earlier, the summation of information on a credit report is calculated through mathematical formulas only known to FICO, and all of the information is boiled down into a single number. This is entirely in your hands to change, as you are not 'branded' with this number.

Each credit bureau will often have a different number assigned to your report, because not all the same information is always reported to all three credit bureaus. Thus a negative reporting account from ABC credit company may show up on a TransUnion Credit Report, but not on Equifax or Experian, and vice versa.

The credit score numbers range from the low 300's to as high as 900. This score range of 300 is considered the 'worst-case scenario ever'. The score range of the upper 800's being considered the 'rarest of the rare' in borrowers, with a perfect credit history.

To even be considered to qualify for a mortgage for a home, a person must have their scores above the mid 600's with most lenders. Borrowers and potential borrowers with numerous negative items on their credit report tend to be in the range between a 450' to 600', depending on their history. If you use this chapter, it is possible to be able to improve your credit score from the low 500's to the 600's or even the mid-700 range quite easily.

The process of having your credit reviewed, and scrutinized can be a disturbing process when you are seeking to obtain financing for a home.

That's why it is highly recommended that you seek to know what is reported on the credit bureau reports before you apply for a mortgage. This can save you a lot of embarrassment and make the process so much more enjoyable.

Prior to the establishment of the FICO scoring system as described in Chapter 2, the loan review process was much more involved and could sometimes be inconsistent. Consequently the door was left open for injustices in the area of financial lending to occur.

Since the Equal Credit Opportunity Act (ECOA), the process has become much more objective. The ECOA states that there cannot be any discrimination in lending based on age (except minors under 18), sex, race, marital status, color, religion, national origin or receipt of public assistance.

In short, when you are reviewing your credit report and trying to improve your credit score, it could best be summarized by saying your scores are based largely on your past performance and your relationships with other creditors. If you failed to pay in a timely manner, as you can see in earlier chapters, this can negatively affect the willingness of other institutions to want to extend you credit.

If you fail to pay altogether, and allow it to go to collections, or bankruptcy, this too will cast a bitter shadow over your history, and further promote to other creditors that lending you money is not such a desirable endeavor. So the past has a profound impact on the future in the world of finance, and has everything to do with buying a home. ECOA makes it a fair playing field for everyone, and you alone are ultimately responsible for your performance and history.

In addition to ECOA, there is another Act that protects you as a consumer. That is the *Fair Credit Reporting Act*. This is a comprehensive Act that covers the ins and outs of financial lending, and establishes a set of rules that must be followed by creditors reporting to credit bureaus. This Act provides for the removal of negative items from the credit report of a consumer, if the consumer can prove what is being reported is not valid.

There are specific rules that must be followed. Essentially if the consumer chooses to dispute an item on his/her credit report to the bureau, the bureau must challenge the creditor. The creditor must then substantiate the negative item within 30 days, or it has to be removed by the credit bureau from the consumers' credit report.

How does one dispute a negative item? You can dispute the items right online when you pull your reports as described in Chapter 3 through www.annualcreditreport.com, or you can write into the credit bureau directly. You can also write the creditor directly and challenge the item on your report.

If the creditor cannot prove the validity of the claim on your report, the credit bureau by law has to remove it per the Fair Credit Reporting Act. It is always a good idea to reference the Fair Credit Reporting Act in any letter you write, as it puts the creditor on alert that you have familiarity with the law.

So how can one go about neutralizing negative items on your credit report?

Well, let's take up a few types of common negative items that can be reported on the credit report:

DELINQUENCY OF ACCOUNTS

Delinquent accounts are perhaps the most common. You missed a payment, sometimes two. The creditor reports you were 30 days late, 60 days late, 90 days late and even 120 days late. These can show up in bright colors if you pull the report online, and they are indicated on little bars that reflect a timeline of usually 2 years on the accounts history. Sometimes the timeline is longer.

Now let's assume you went through Chapter 2, and decided to change some of the ways you have been doing things. Let's also assume, you gained a better understanding of what constitutes good behavior on credit from reading Chapter 3. Is it possible that you have since improved your consistency on the way you manage your accounts, and have improved your performance on the monthly payments on your existing accounts, and you haven't been late recently?

Maybe it's been quite some time since you were late, and you have structured your life to never be late again. Perhaps what is showing up on the report happened several months to a year ago, and you have recovered since then, but these 30-

60-90's are hanging fire on your credit score. It is easier to demonstrate a case example of how one man handled this problem on his credit report, and the results from doing so. Here is his story:

In 1999 Mr. Smith moved with his wife from Florida to Missouri, after selling his company to two partners as part of a separation of partnership. Having to relocate to Missouri on a job transfer for his wife, Mr. Smith had to leave earlier than expected before finalizing all the sale of partnership documentation. The result was that the ultimate sale of the company carried on for 2 years, before it was finally brought to closure in 2001.

During this time, Mr. Smith fell delinquent on several credit cards, and had accumulated a series of 30-60-90's on ten separate credit cards for a period lasting 18 months. In 2004 after he had recovered financially, and paid off all his creditors through the sale of his company, he finally pulled his credit scores online and saw the damage to his reports. Although the debts were paid, the delinquency reports still remained.

In reviewing his credit report, he discovered that the creditor reporting on one of his accounts had misidentified the dates when he was late, according to his records. Another account was found to be similar. He decided to dispute this with the two creditors. He sent them a letter challenging the entirety of their reported information, based on the premise that if they were wrong on this one date, maybe they were off on the others as well. Not having all of his own records, but having enough to create a suspicion, he challenged their reporting with 'What you are reporting does not match my records'.

After 30 days, both creditors wrote him back with answers. One creditor could no longer find records of his account, having switched computer systems two years earlier, and removed the entire delinquency history. This removed a series of four 30 day late reports, two 60 day late reports, and one 90 day late report entirely from his credit report. The second creditor was only able to substantiate one of the 30 days late periods, and removed the remainder. This removed four 30 day late periods, and one 60 day late that was being reported.

Suddenly his credit report took on a whole

new picture. He decided to write the remaining eight remaining creditors, and also write the credit bureaus at the same time as sort of a double whammy. He merely followed his same pattern of investigation, and compared his records with what was being reported and found enough discrepancies to comfortably feel he could substantiate a challenge. So he wrote his letters with the same dispute information, indicating that what they were reporting did not match his records, and requesting politely for the items to be removed.

The result was that all eight either deleted the entire account history, or cleaned the report up to reflect that there were no delinquencies for their entire history! The various reasons that caused this change were many. Three creditors could no longer find the account records, having upgraded their database. One company no longer existed, having been bought out by another credit card company. Another never responded to the credit bureaus in a timely manner, so the bureaus removed it from the reports. The remainder just removed it without a challenge.

So in summary, from 2004 through 2005, Mr. Smith cleaned his three credit reports up from having forty separate 30-60-90 day delinquencies reported by ten separate accounts to having just one 30 day delinquency reported by one account. His credit score rose from the mid 600's to the mid 700's in a few months.

The important point to remember on this is that Mr. Smith first changed his behavior on how he handled his credit accounts, and then sought to clean up the picture presented of his past on the credit reports. It is entirely unethical to falsify information you report to a credit bureau, and could get you into some serious legal trouble if you do.

So contact a competent Financial Planner or an Attorney familiar with this area if you have any questions regarding this. This case example was given to you to show how conflicting records that you can prove can be disputed, and the potential results that could be forthcoming. I cannot stress enough the importance of getting in your own personal financial organization, as I discussed in Chapter 2, prior to taking this step.

Now let's look at some other items that can be reported as negative on a credit report.

COLLECTION ACCOUNTS

Collection accounts are debt that were failed to be paid, and were sent to a collection agency or department to collect, and they in turn reported the debt on your credit reports.

The first and best way to remove these items from your credit report if they are valid is to pay them. If they are old (say older than 2 years), many times you can get in touch with the original creditor and pay them directly or negotiate a settlement for less. It may also be a solution for you to roll these kinds of debts into some other line of credit so they can be removed from the credit report. A financial advisor can help you explore the various options regarding this, depending on the size of the debt. By financial advisor, I mean a Certified Public Accountant, an Attorney or an expert trained in the procedure for credit report repair.

Always get the agreement from the creditor to remove this from your credit report once settled, and get it in writing. When you receive the written proof that the debt was settled, or 'paid in-full', make copies. Keep one copy for your records, and send in a letter with the attached proof of payment to the credit bureaus that are reporting this on your credit report. Do not assume that the credit collection department will take the extra steps to see that it is removed from your credit reports, just because you paid them or the person you spoke with verbally told you they would take care of it. Many times they do not do this, and old debts that were in fact paid continue to be reported on your credit report, and this can negatively affect your score.

If you do come across items that you in fact paid on the report, then the best route to take is to dispute this with the credit bureaus and send along proof of payment. If you can't find proof of payment, then dispute it anyway, and by causing the credit bureau to challenge the credit collection agency, as this may result in getting it removed.

PUBLIC RECORDS

Public records can cover many things: Judgments, Foreclosures, Court Fees, Delinquent Child Support or Alimony, etc. Essentially any indebtedness enforced by the court systems, and placed on your credit report.

The best and first rule of thumb on any debt is to pay them. However, there can be certain cases where debts show up that are not valid. In most of these cases, it is best to consult with an attorney to get these removed, corrected or resolved. I have known of many cases where the legal process was not followed in accordance with the written law, and items have been removed from public record as a result.

Once again, if you have proof that a debt has been settled, or evidence that it is not your debt, then this can be disputed through the credit bureaus by providing the evidence and requesting removal.

CHARGE-OFFS

'Charge-offs' are debts that the creditor has in most cases written off as bad debt, and not sought further collection. They have just noted the unpaid debt on the credit report, and it continues to taint your credit report until it falls off or is removed.

Following the best course of action, I will recommend that you contact the creditor reporting this and attempt to pay the debt to resolve this or negotiate a settlement. Once again, get any settlement in writing and request they remove the item from your credit report.

If for some reason the creditor that reported this cannot be contacted, will not respond, or no longer exists, dispute the negative item with the credit bureau and request that it be removed. Generally charge-offs will remain on your credit report for seven years.

BANKRUPTCIES

Bankruptcies can hold down a credit score. The best solution I can recommend is to clean up the rest of the credit report, if there are any negative items, as a first action. Bankruptcies, unlike other items on a credit report, are not likely to be removed. There are credit repair specialists that have had success on getting these removed in some cases where the exact legal procedure was not followed in the bankruptcies execution.

Bankruptcies are recorded by date of

'discharge' from the courts. The best recommendation for those that have a bankruptcy on their record is to keep a clean present and future credit performance, and work to clean up any other potentially negative items as discussed earlier.

A bankruptcy is not going to prevent you from getting financed on a loan, but it does limit your options on programs and interest rates that will be made available to you. So the cleaner you can keep you current payment history, and the rest of your report, the better. You increase your credit score in other ways, by doing so, and work around the bankruptcy until it eventually falls off the report.

Most current loan programs require a bankruptcy to be older than two years from the date of discharge. The farther back in your history the better.

Bankruptcies filed under Chapter 7 or Chapter 11 will stay on a credit report ten years. Bankruptcies filed under Chapter 13 will stay on a credit report generally seven years.

MYSTERY DEBT

By far the most alarming discovery to find on your credit report is a charge or delinquent account that you have no clue as to what it is or how it got under your name. I call this section 'Mystery Debt', for lack of a better name. I have included this section, as it is inevitable that I come across someone that pulls their credit reports and discovers debt that is being reported that they have no knowledge of. This can occur in many forms. Mistaken identity, divorce settlement misreporting of debt, a wrongly entered social security number, outright fraud, and co-signing a loan with someone and forgetting all about it are among the common reasons. There can be many other reasons. Ultimately if the debt is not yours, then it should not be on your credit report, and you will have to make this known to the credit bureaus.

The best route is to dispute, dispute, and then dispute again. Send letters to the credit bureaus and creditors reporting such, as a first action. Re-dispute again and again with more information each time until it is removed. If it is a case of identity theft, report it as such, and put it in writing to the credit bureaus so it can be investigated.

If it does not get removed, and it is determined to be a case of fraud, you can report it as such to the credit bureaus. If this does not resolve it, report it the Federal Bureau of Investigation (FBI) and provide all the information. The FBI has a division that specializes in credit fraud and they are keenly interested in tracking down this kind crime. There is usually a regional FBI office, and you can usually obtain contact information through your local police department.

HARD-LINE CREDIT REPAIR

I recommend doing whatever you can to clean up errors yourself first, and then when all else fails consult with one of these companies, if your credit score is still too low to qualify for a loan. There are companies, however, that offer 'Hard-line' Credit repair services, or sometimes called 'Hard-core' credit repair services. They charge fees, and in some cases it's a good investment as these organizations can sometimes remove and clean up unmovable items on the credit report.

These companies that have a proven record have been known to successfully remove foreclosures, collections, delinquent accounts, judgment, charge-offs and all manner of reported debt. Depending on the amount of repair needed on a credit report, these companies will charge usually from as low as a few hundred dollars to several thousand. It all depends on the amount of work that is involved in this process. You can also be expected to pay for fees in advance.

As you can see, much of the credit repair process can be done successfully on your own with very little expense involved. It does require patience, planning and once again getting in a basic organization system to prevent the past from repeating itself.

Realize that you must address all three credit bureaus, as it is not enough to simply clean up one report. Many lenders pull all three credit bureau reports, and will choose the middle score of the three. So if you only go through the trouble of fixing one report, you could still have a low score on the other two and not qualify for the better loan programs.

It is also important to remember that if an item is reported only on one bureau report. Only dispute something that is with just the bureau that is reporting it only, and not the other two.

You would not want to worsen your situation by having these other two bureaus investigate the debt, and get it substantiated, and then add it to your credit report with them. So be careful to dispute with only those bureaus that are reporting the specific negative item. You will avoid a lot of headache.

SUMMARIZING CREDIT REPAIR

Many of the common negative items on credit reports can be cleaned up in 30 to 90 days, and, at the most, 6 months. Removing as many negative items as possible can greatly increase your overall score. Consider that your credit score can affect the interest rate you receive on your loan, this is time well invested. A higher interest rate due to a lower credit score can cost you several tens of thousands to hundreds of thousands of dollars on the life of your loan. This can mean the difference of hundreds of dollars on your monthly payments. A little preparation and research can go a long way towards making homeownership more enjoyable in the long run.

In summary, the following is a list of negatives to neutralize if they exist:

- Delinquent Accounts

- Unpaid Collection Accounts

- Public Records

- Charge-Offs

- Bankruptcies

- "Mystery Debt"

These are the areas that will cause the bulk of the trouble on a credit report, and should be corrected, paid off and removed as appropriate before you fill out a loan application and have your credit report pulled by a lender.

OPTIONS FOR SCENARIOS WHERE THE CREDIT REPAIR MAY TAKE 3 TO 5 YEARS

What if your credit repair process is going to take three to five years because of the amount of issues you have to resolve on your credit report? What if you are dealing with an automobile repossession that occurred five years ago and will need a few more years to fall off your credit report? What if you had a foreclosure or bankruptcy in the last two years? These issues, although sometimes resolvable, can weigh heavy on a credit report.

There are basically five main options in this case that are available to you:

1) Save, and purchase a home for outright cash. Then re-finance later after your credit is repaired if you want to pull the cash back out.

2) Purchase a home that is being made available on Land Contract or Contract for Deed. (For more about how this works, see my book: Understanding Land Contract Homes: In Pursuit of the American Dream) Re-finance the home later on at a specified time defined

in the agreement called a 'balloon' payment.

3) Purchase a home with a lease with an option to buy. A lease with an option to buy is essentially a lease agreement where you place a down payment called an 'option' which give you the option of purchasing a home a specified price within a designated period of time. The option payment gets applied to the down payment when you purchase. If you do not purchase it, the option payment can be non-refundable depending on how the contract is written.

4) Find an individual (usually a family member or close friend) who will buy the home for you and either hold a private mortgage or arrange a land contract agreement to sell it back to you with interest on their investment. Re-finance later when you have your credit repaired.

5) There are also private charity organizations such as 'Habitat for Humanity' that sometimes offer programs to help you privately finance a house.

In various other markets around the country, there may be other variations on this that you can apply, but this is generally the four options you have available to you.

Otherwise, you should work on cleaning up what you can on your credit report and perhaps new lending programs will be made available to you.

Chapter Five:

Getting Approved for Financing

After having corrected your finances past and present, it is time to examine the next step in the process of buying a home. Many times the best place to look for financing is your very own bank, credit union or savings and loan that you do business with regularly. This is always a good place to start. However, I will caution you on the fact that if you have gotten this far in the process and have a good credit score, you owe it to yourself to shop around

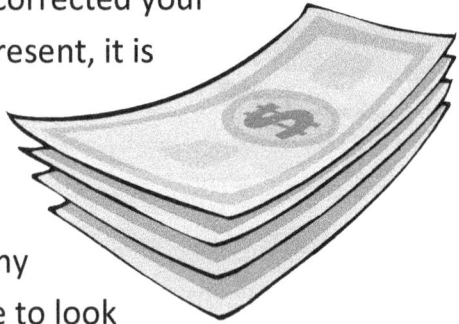

to at least three places.

The first one being your own financial institution, the next two should be recommended to you by your Real Estate Agent. Why a Real Estate Agent? For the simple reason, it is their business to have an excellent familiarity with the cutting edge loan programs in the industry and will work with you on the best options for your circumstances.

If you go to one lender specifically, you will only have exposure to the programs that that firm offers. So seek someone who can offer you some direction, and your best resource is your Real Estate Agent. There are some lenders that can offer only a few specific loan programs, and there are others that can offer many. You will want to explore options in both conventional loans, and the variety of government loan programs that you might qualify for.

If you do not have a Real Estate Agent, find one. Who should your choose? The best answer: *Someone you feel comfortable working with.* You can also seek a referral for one from a friend or family member you trust. Make sure it is someone you enjoy working with, as it is important to find someone that listens and understands what you are looking for so that you can arrive at your goal. A few great online source websites to find agents is the: Council of Residential Specialists *www.crs.com* and the Real Estate Buyers Agent Council *www.Rebac.com*. More will be described on these organizations in the next chapter.

The next professional you will need is a Loan Officer. Who or what is a Loan Officer? A Loan Officer is someone in the business of originating and processing mortgage loan applications, and are the representative between you and the 'lenders' or 'underwriters', the ones who actually loan the money. A Loan Officer can be from your bank, savings and loan, or an independent mortgage brokerage office. It is the lenders representative you will be working with through the financing portion of the process.

The process for approval is quite easy if you have already addressed and resolved negative items on your credit report. It is also a breeze if you have a good credit score for the program you are applying for. It becomes as easy as filling out a loan application, and receiving an approval letter. Loan Officers can do this today by using a system called the 'Automated Underwriting System'. Underwriting is defined as: *"A process of matching a borrower's credit and income history with a very rigid set of standards, which is not deviated from except in very rare circumstances."*

Historically this was usually sent to a committee that was typically very conservative. A committee could sometimes take 1-2 weeks depending on the volume of applications they have to review. Today, the world has become computerized. What took weeks before, takes literally seconds with the Automated Underwriting System (AUS).

THE AUTOMATED UNDERWRITING SYSTEM

Loan Officers using this system can input the information from your credit application and credit bureau reports, and have a complete summary of the programs you qualify for within a matter of seconds.

Automated Underwriting Systems (AUS) are computer programs with the ability to consider all variables in making a decision of loan approval or denial. These systems can objectively take into account all strengths and weaknesses of the borrower.

The AUS matches all minimum standards of a specific loan program with the borrower's information from the application and input data. The AUS is also able to take into account any compensating factors such as savings and retirement accounts which could be used to make mortgage payments during difficult times for the borrower.

Other items such as job stability are accounted for, which can assist in overcoming shortfalls. The AUS is able to take into consideration all of the borrowers variables in generating a loan decision. The AUS can generate a loan decision in literally seconds from start to finish.

So in the age of the computer, the long drawn out approval process is no more. Whenever I have found someone having difficulty with an approval process, it is because they usually have to resolve issues on their credit report or giving more details to improve the financial presentation on the application before it reaches the underwriting department of a lender.

This is where an experienced Loan Officer can help you navigate through the difficulties. It also is important to recognize that if you truly addressed any negative credit issues as covered earlier, then you will not have to address them with your loan officer or lender. That is where preparation before you meet with the Loan Officer is vital, as covered in the preceding chapters.

Here is a list of basic criteria that is examined or asked about usually in the process of applying for a loan. This is just a summary, and there can be more than this, depending on the loan program and changes in lending regulations, etc.

➢ Income (Depending on the program, the criteria usually is they want to see you earn 3X to 4X as much as your estimated monthly mortgage payment will be.)

➢ Length of time at current employment (They want to see 2+ years usually).

➢ Credit Score

- Credit History

- Savings, Retirement Accounts (IRA's, 401K's, etc.) and other reserves.

- Assets (These can be material items as well as stocks, bonds, etc.)

- Liabilities (Debts and obligations you already are committed to)

- Whether you have owned a home in the last 2-5 years (Certain first time home buyer criteria will have this is as a requirement).

- Military Records (With VA loans this information will need to be provided, for example).

- Tax Records

THE PRE-APPROVAL LETTER

Once all criteria is examined, and it is determined you have met the basic criteria, the Loan Officer will write a 'Pre-Approval Letter' from their company stating that you have been 'pre-approved' for financing. This will usually indicate the terms of your financing program on it. Once you have this pre-approval letter, you will also have an idea of the price range of home you should be shopping for.

Additionally, you will have specific directions from your lender on the program you have selected, and this information will be vital for your Real Estate Agent to know in helping you to write and negotiate an offer on a home you select.

A pre-approval letter is not a guarantee of financing; it merely approves you for a specific loan program. You still have to go through the loan qualification process, and this usually is done once an offer to buy a home is written and a copy is submitted to your lender so that the agreed upon terms of the offer can be sent to underwriting for approval, along with the examination, appraisal and details of the home you are purchasing. This process is often called the 'loan origination' process by lenders.

Often a pre-approval letter will define what is called a 'rate lock-in' period. This is simply a specified amount of time a lender has guaranteed a particular interest rate to a borrower. This means that in order to get the loan at the defined interest rate, the borrower must have selected a home, have a signed purchase contract by the seller and gotten all the documents to the lender in order to close on the loan within a specified time period. To receive the locked in interest rate, one must close the loan by a specific deadline.

A Pre-approval letter is usually submitted with any offer to purchase, which provides a statement of validity in the financing behind the offer. An 'Offer to Purchase' or 'Purchase Contract' is a contract written with the help of a Real Estate Agent which defines the terms you as a potential 'buyer' are offering for the purchase of the house. It will include your requirements for financing, as well as defining who is responsible for the various fees in the transaction, either buyer or seller.

This is where your Real Estate Agent can be of a great assistance to you, as they are quite familiar with the process and can help you avoid costly mistakes. Real Estate Agents are trained in the negotiation process, and have a unique understanding of the market. They can advise you whether terms in the contract or the condition of the house will have an impact on your pre-approved financing. They will also coordinate with your Loan Officer to make certain that any offer is written to reflect the loan programs defined in the pre-approval letter.

APPLICATION FEES

When applying for a loan, lenders usually charge a fee to process the application. This fee covers the lenders cost of processing the application, and is often non-refundable. They may also require you to pay in advance for the appraisal, so you will want to ask about these fees early on in the process so that you can be prepared.

METHODS OF LOANING MONEY

There are two methods of loaning money for real estate. They are either through the use of a 'Mortgage' or a 'Deed of Trust'. There are distinct, yet simple differences between the two.

A 'Mortgage' is defined as: A financial arrangement wherein an individual borrows money to purchase real property and secures the loan using the property as collateral.

A 'Deed of Trust' is defined as: Property is

transferred to a trustee by a borrower ('trustor', or creator of the legal 'trust'), in favor of the lender (beneficiary), and the re-conveyed to the borrower upon payment in full.

In essence the difference between the two is who holds the deed to the property. The type of loan used will vary from State to State throughout the U.S. The method that is used will depend on which State you are buying the property. Your loan officer or Real Estate Agent will be able to tell you which method is used by the State you are buying a home in.

SOME COMMON LOAN PROGRAMS

There are many loan programs in existence. I have put together a short list of definitions of four of the common types of programs you are more likely to hear about. There are variations on each one, and some may define the type of home you can buy to use that loan. One should consult with a qualified Loan Officer to find the program that best meets their needs, as well as a review of the complete summary of loan programs available.

CONVENTIONAL LOAN PROGRAMS: This is

essentially a mortgage or deed of trust not obtained under a government loan program. These loans are financed by independently owned, non-government agencies.

FHA LOAN PROGRAMS: The acronym 'FHA' stands for 'Federal Housing Administration' which is a sub-agency of the U.S. Department of Housing and Urban Development (HUD) created in the 1930's to facilitate the purchase of homes by low income, first time home buyers. The federal agency insures the first mortgage, and enables lenders to loan a very high percentage of the sales price of a home.

USDA 'RURAL DEVELOPMENT' LOAN PROGRAMS: This is another loan program administered by the US Department of Agriculture to facilitate lending in rural areas. The qualifications to the borrower are similar to an FHA loan, however the property must be located within the parameters of the USDA maps that define rural areas.

VA GUARANTEE LOAN PROGRAMS: The acronym 'VA' stands for 'Veterans Administration'. This government agency is responsible for ensuring the rights and welfare of our nation's veterans and their dependants. Among other duties, the VA insures home loans made to veterans and the VA Guarantee program is main program at this time. Years of service and type of service come into play with qualifying for this, and one can look at the VA website for more details.

With all loan programs there are variations, and it is useful time well spent in learning as much as you can about the nuances and benefits of the ones that appeal to you.

More information on these, and other lending terms is made available in the reference sections at the back of this book. Loan programs change with the times, as well as requirements and funding, so consult with a Loan Officer that can offer you a variety of programs to find the best one for you.

Chapter Six:

Hunting for Your Dream Home

Now that you are pre-approved, it's time for some real fun! The thrill of the hunt begins! Finding that dream home! The place you will not only start a new life with, but you will put the world of renting behind you.

The pre-approval letter from your lender will usually give you a price range that you should be shopping in for a new home. The type of loan program may also define what condition the home can be in, and as in USDA Rural Development loans, the location.

Now the question that sometimes comes to the table is 'Why do I need a Real Estate Agent?' In other words, why not just go look for a house and approach the homeowner and give them a verbal offer, come to an agreement and boom! I have a deal!

THE SELLERS REPRESENTATIVE

In almost any market in the U.S. a greater majority of the homes for sale are being listed through a Real Estate Agent. The reason is that Real Estate Agents are the experts in marketing and selling homes. They are the licensed professionals in the industry of selling homes.

The Real Estate Agent is paid with a commission for doing so, which is either a fixed fee or more commonly an agreed upon percentage of the asking price. There is a legal contract binding the seller to the Real Estate Agent called an 'Exclusive Listing Contract'. This is a contract between the owner of the property and the Real Estate Agent giving the agent the exclusive right to sell the property. One sells a home, a Real Estate Agent is contacted and then contracted to sell it and vice versa.

So if you approach a seller who has their home listed through a Real Estate Agent, you will be directed to speak with their agent to present any offers. They are the hired professional representing the sellers, also known as the 'Sellers Representative'.

Listing Real Estate Agents many times offer a part or percentage of the commission to another agent who represents a buyer. When there is no other Real Estate Agent involved, the listing agent retains the full commission from the sale.

So if you are not represented by a Real Estate Agent, and you approach a listing Real Estate Agent, he will help you write the offer and submit it to his seller for review. The point that is often overlooked by the buyer in this case is that the listing agent is not representing you as the buyer. They are working for and representing *the seller*.

Any offer he/she helps you write and negotiate is to benefit the *seller*, as they are not representing you. You may still get a great deal, but the primary obligation is to the seller of the property, not you as the buyer in this case. This is a common misunderstanding buyers sometimes have. They believe that because the listing agent is offering to help them write the offer, that they are somehow represented in the transaction. In fact, they are not. However, there is a solution to this.

THE BUYERS' REPRESENTATIVE

When working with a Real Estate Agent if you are a potential buyer, there is a relationship called 'Buyer's Agency'. This is where you sign an agreement with a Real Estate Agent to represent you as a *buyer*. A 'Buyer's Agent' or 'Buyer's Representative' can be paid in two ways.

You as the buyer can pay his or her commission as part of your closing costs, or he/she can get paid from the seller through the sale of the home.

This is often indicated in the marketing of a listing by the listing agent as to whether the seller and listing agent are agreeable to pay a buyer's agent commission. In either case, the commission is going to get paid on any listed property, and so it is in your best interest to solicit the help of a Real Estate Agent, and have someone working for you.

The advantage of a Real Estate Agent working for you is that they are looking out for your interests throughout the transaction, and will often help you avoid mistakes that you might regret in the long term. The negotiation becomes more in your favor, especially in a market where there are a lot of homes for sale, sometimes called a 'Buyer's Market'.

The opposite of this is a 'Seller's Market'. This is where there are more buyers than sellers. In this kind of market, it is also important to have buyer representation as one has to obtain information rapidly, and move fast on any offer to purchase. This makes the buyer's agent's role vital, as they have access to this cutting edge information in such a tight market.

If you wait for the newspaper advertising in a 'seller's market' the house could already be sold. The economy of real estate goes through cycles, and can see many changes in a market over a decade.

Your Real Estate Agent is the best resource to keep you informed of the local real estate market, as they have their finger on the pulse in their daily work.

THE NATIONAL ASSOCIATION OF REALTORS®

Professional Real Estate Agents in the U.S. are licensed through a National Organization called 'The National Association of REALTORS®'(NAR). Licensed Real Estate Agents hold the professional designation of 'REALTOR®'.

They are also licensed through their State Association, as well as their local Board, which is also regulated through NAR.

In choosing a REALTOR® to work with, as I described in the last chapter, you will want to choose someone you are comfortable working with. You might consider seeking advice from a friend or family member as a referral. Be sure whomever you choose is a licensed REALTOR®, and are a

member of the National Association of REALTORS®
(NAR).

NAR enforces a strict ethics code of practice
for all who hold the REALTOR® designation, so you
can be sure you are working with a professional.
You can search for members of NAR on their
website: *www.realtor.com*

THE COUNCIL OF RESIDENTIAL SPECIALISTS

Another organization
endorsed by NAR that you can
also consult with is the 'Council
of Residential Specialists (CRS)'.
This organization instructs already
licensed REALTORS® on advanced training, and
offers a certification to REALTORS® who meet the
criteria entitled 'CERTIFIED RESIDENTIAL
SPECIALIST' (CRS). To obtain the CRS designation, a
REALTOR® is required to take over 50 hours of
advanced training, as well as sell 25 homes or more
to qualify. The advanced training required for the
CRS designation requires passing a rigorous
examination, and the courses often require out-of-
state travel to attend. So a REALTOR® that is willing

to do this demonstrates a profound and serious commitment to being on the cutting edge of their profession. This is a great pool of resources for locating and selecting an experienced REALTOR®, as you already know they have sold many homes and they have advanced training beyond other agents.

THE REAL ESTATE BUYERS' AGENT COUNCIL

Another organization that offers advanced training for REALTORS® is the 'Real Estate Buyers Agent Council (REBAC)' which offers special training for REALTORS® that specialize in 'Buyers Agency'. The designation they offer is called 'Accredited Buyer Representative' or ABR. The ABR designation requires approximately 30 hours of advanced training and the sale of at least 5 houses as a 'Buyers Representative' to qualify.

So if you do not have a REALTOR®, and your friends don't have a referral for you, then contact either or both of these organizations and find a REALTOR® with this special training and you will get someone with proven experience. Some REALTORS® will often have both of these designations.

You can search these organizations websites at:

Council of Residential Specialists:
www.crs.com

Real Estate Buyers Agent Council:
www.rebac.net

Both of these sites offer searches for your geographic area for those agents with their designations. There are many other types of designations for REALTORS® that you can find information about on the National Association of Realtors website: *www.Realtor.com*

FAIR HOUSING

Unfair housing practices are prohibited by both federal and state laws across the United States. In summary, this prohibits anyone in the profession of

EQUAL HOUSING OPPORTUNITY

real estate, or mortgage lending from refusing to negotiate for or engage in a real estate transaction with a person because of race, color, religion, national origin, age, sex, familial status, marital status, or mental and physical handicap.

In some states, this list is further expanded to include height, weight, sexual orientation and HIV Positive. Discrimination in the terms of a rental, lease, or purchase is against the law. It also includes in the furnishing of facilities in connection with such as a transaction, such as appraising a home, property inspections, land surveys, etc. This also extends to publishing or advertising, directly or indirectly, or intent to make a limitation, specification or discrimination based on any of the categories listed above.

The origin of these civil rights goes back to the Civil Rights Act of 1866. It was later expanded with the Civil Rights Act of 1968, and the later the 'Persons with Disabilities Civil Rights Act' of 1976. Many states have followed with their own civil rights acts pertaining to each state constitution.

In summary, these rights should be known to you as a homebuyer, as they are your rights. In the

Real Estate profession, there is a symbol for 'Equal Housing Opportunity' that is displayed on advertising and promotional materials by Real Estate firms:

This symbol indicates they are seeking to protect your rights, and their offices are in compliance with the laws.

NARROWING THE FOCUS

Now you have chosen a REALTOR® to work with, what next?

Before you go house shopping, especially when there are a lot of homes for sale, you should take time to make a short list of what you are looking for in a home.

The following is a short checklist to go through to help you narrow the list of available homes to look at:

- What City or area of town would you like to live in?

- How big of a home do you want in terms of square footage?

- How many bedrooms?

- How many bathrooms?

- Do you want a garage?

- If you want a garage: how many cars?

- What size of a yard do you want, if any?

- Do you want acreage?

- How about a basement?

- Swimming pool?

- How about the size of the rooms?

- Do you want a fireplace?

- What about the style of the house?

- Do you want waterfront property?

- Do you want a rural, suburban or urban location?

- Is there a preferred school district you would like to be in?

- Do you want to be in a gated

community?

With these beginning criteria already decided, it is possible to narrow the focus of what types of properties you are looking for. A Realtor can literally take the answers to above questions and punch in a search criteria to the local Multiple Listing Service (MLS) to pull up a list of properties that meet these general specifications. The MLS is a computerized database used by Realtors, and contains a complete inventory of all the homes listed for sale in a given area. This detailed searching will give you a more direct list of homes you are inclined to like, and help you narrow your selection down to a handful of favorites.

Once you have your initial list, your Realtor can print out specification sheets or flyers on each property complete with photographs so you can look through them and choose which ones you want to see first. This is a fast and simple way to further narrow down the selection. You may find that the photograph of a home does not appeal to you first off, so you put this one to the bottom of the list. Or you see one that pops your eyes out, and makes all the bells go off, so you put this one on your must see list. Your Realtor can then set up the appointments for you to see each of these homes, usually all in the same time frame according to your available schedule.

TOURING THE HOMES YOU SELECT

Touring the homes is the next vital step. When you visit it, make a note of all the points that appeal to you and the ones that don't. Ask some general questions of yourself: Is the home 'move-in ready' or will you require repairs be made before you can move in? If it requires work, is it something you don't mind doing? Can you picture in your mind's eye where your furniture would go? You might have numerous other questions you can think of that are important to you. Your Realtor can also be a valuable resource in helping you sort through the decision making process.

There is no universal magic formula for choosing a perfect home. The best advice one can give on this is to look at several homes, and re-visit the ones you are most interested in. Make your decision based on what you want, and whether the house meets the criteria for you or not.

The reverse can also be true. I have run into people shopping for a home that are seeking the 'perfect' house. In truth, there is no *'perfect'* house, and perfection is a relative subject privy to the eyes of the beholder. So the pendulum can swing both ways, and what is most important is: do you like the house enough to live there? Would you honestly enjoy living there? Does it meet a majority of your needs? Will it fit into your long term lifestyle and plans? In the end, that is really all that matters.

The selection process can take some time, or it can be very short. Being prepared to act upon a house that meets your needs when you see it can be instrumental in determining the length of this process. If you hesitate too long on a good house, it might not be available the next time you decide to see it.

Let's put it into perspective. Imagine you will see as many as 20 houses, and one of these 20 will ultimately be the one you buy. Recognize that the house you are looking for could be the 1st, or the 2nd one you see, or the 20th, or anywhere in between. Being confident enough to skip the other

18 when you know it is right takes discipline. This comes from knowing more of what you are looking for before you start your search, so you can spend less time looking at the wrong houses.

Having this worked out beforehand will help you make a confident final decision. Often indecision and procrastination when shopping for a new home, is the primary delay. This contributes to a long drawn out hunting process. So be alert and ready to make your offer when the right house that meets your specifications comes along. Additionally in a competitive buying market, passing up on a perfect house to see a few more later in the week could mean that someone else gets an offer in before you, and the home is no longer available.

So place yourself in a frame of mind to decide quickly and either place an offer, or move on without regret. Thought is an instantaneous thing, so when someone decides they need to 'think about it' they really skipping the initial step of defining the criteria of what they are looking for, and measuring what they are looking at against that criteria. There is really nothing more to that. That is all hesitation really is in this process, the omission of sorting out in advance what it important to you. It will also help to share this information with your Realtor, as they can narrow the homes they show you to fit within these parameters and in so doing, show you homes you are more likely to love.

CAN ONE ALSO SEARCH FOR HOMES ONLINE?

With the age and growth of the internet, there are many online places to search for homes in your area. Often I will be working with clients with who are interested in buying a home, and find listed homes on websites such as: *Trulia.com, Homes.com* or *Zillow.com*.

These website are good resources, but they do have a particular flaw which many prospective buyers do not realize. The information on the properties are pulled from the internet when a home goes for sale, but they often do not have any more information than that. A prospective buyer can find a home they love on one of those websites, and be frequently disappointed to learn that it is under contract with another buyer or already sold.

Also, homes on that website are uploaded on a delay, so if the home is in a high demand area it can many times be sold before it goes live on one of these websites.

So what can a buyer do it they want to shop for more current online information? Realtors have access to a system mentioned earlier called the 'Multiple Listing Service' (MLS) and this information is online. Depending on what area of the country you are in, and the web software platform that Realtor MLS information is made available, your Realtor can provide you with this information in some fashion as new homes hit the market. They can set you up with an instant email of new listings within your criteria or location, or give you access to the search the public side of their MLS if it is available. This is the best way to get access to current homes for sale, and be on the cutting edge of the active homes on the market.

With such an arrangement in place between you and your agent, you can see homes almost as instantly as they hit the market. This will give you a first look and opportunity to see the homes you are most interested in. If you wait for these other online sites, you can often be chasing homes that have already been shown to other buyers as much as a week before you see it. So take advantage of your working relationship with a Realtor in your area, and you will have the edge over other buyers in a competitive market.

Once you have hunted and found your dream home, the next step is to write the offer.

Chapter Seven:

OFFERING WHAT IS RIGHT

This chapter is about offering what is right for a property, and writing the right offer.

Before you write an offer, ask your Realtor to do a *'Comparative Market Analysis'* or CMA on the home you have selected. A CMA is a comparison of similar homes that have sold in that area, usually within the last year, so that a comparison can be done to the existing home to determine a price. If the asking price is higher that the medium of the CMA, in most cases the home is over-priced.

The comparison, however, must include

comparing apples to apples, so you would not want to compare a home of the same square footage that is vastly different in condition and amenities to the home you are considering buying.

There is a definite difference between 'Appraisal Value' and 'Fair Market Value' in Real Estate. 'Appraisal Value' is derived at by an appraiser that is trained to examine the structure of the property, and give a recommendation of value from his experience and training. He draws from sales information and tax records to assign a value, as does a Realtor. However, appraisers can err if they are unfamiliar with current market conditions, or come from outside the market area.

'Fair Market Value' is strictly driven by the sales of homes in the given area. A thorough CMA researched and compiled by a Realtor will give you the market value of the home. It will give you an index of what the market is willing to pay for a home.

An appraisal value is an appraiser's opinion on the value of the home. This can vary in many situations. For example, if the appraiser is called in by a bank from another city, he may not be familiar enough with the local market value, and could err by giving an appraised value too high or too low basing it on their familiarity with their own market.

This is not common, but it has been known to happen. Fair Market Value should be the price estimate you seek, as this is based on sales of the recent market in that neighborhood or area, and it will give you a better index. However, a loan will require an appraisal, so it is important to remember that. A CMA can guide you as to whether a home is likely to appraise at the offered price.

One can also have a projected market value from a CMA. This might be a value of the home, once repairs and upgrades are done to bring it up to the comparative value of homes in the neighborhood. So even a home that is a 'fixer-upper' can be evaluated as to price, before and after upgrades and repairs are done. For example, a listed home you are interested in has been foreclosed on previously by a bank.

The foreclosed home is in a visibly neglected condition, but it has 3 bedrooms, 1 bath and a 2 car garage and is being listed for $40,000 in its present condition. The CMA for similar homes in the area in good condition, with the same number of rooms, is $80,000 to $90,000, so you have a potentially great buy.

Once you have your CMA, and it checks out, and you are happy with the home, it becomes time to put together an offer. You Realtor through the use of a CMA can help you determine a fair price to offer. This could be the exact price being asked in the listing price, or it could be less, and in some cases more.

If your loan program described on your approval letter from your lender indicates that you should include a request for seller contribution to financing in any offer you write, then this will need to be contemplated in how the offer is written. A 'Seller Contribution' is essentially the seller incurring part or all of the closing costs, and in certain programs, the down payment the buyer needs to purchase the home.

For example, if your lender requires that you get 3% of the purchase price of the home from the seller as a contribution (also called a concession) towards closing costs, the offer you write will need to include this. This might be a case where you offer 3% more than what is being asked in the listing price to the seller, in return for 3% contribution towards closing costs.

You will only want to do this if there is equity in the home. What this means is that the market value you and your Realtor determined for the home is higher than what they are asking for in the sales price. This kind of negotiation is why it is very important to have a Realtor, especially one experienced in the lending process.

INSPECTIONS

Your offer to purchase should also include reserving the right to have the property inspected. This would include any inspections or testing required in your State or area, and should include structural, plumbing, electrical, HVAC, termite, radon, mold, etc. If it a rural property on a well and/or septic system, you will want to include those also. Usually there is a time frame for doing these inspections, and they begin when the seller agrees and signs on acceptance of your offer. This window of time may only be ten days, and this is not ten working days, but ten calendar days. So be prepared to act quickly.

THE EARNEST OR 'GOOD FAITH' DEPOSIT

You should also be prepared to put down an earnest deposit (sometimes called a 'good faith' deposit) with your offer. This can vary in price, depending on the size of the property you are purchasing. Your Realtor will be able to advise you on the recommended amount to include with the offer to purchase. The earnest deposit makes it a binding contract once the offer is accepted, and in many States you cannot have a contract without one.

THE BASIC STRUCTURE OF YOUR OFFER

So in essence, your offer will be structured around information provided by your lender, will include a right to inspect and also an earnest deposit as a minimum. There can be many additional things negotiated in a contract for purchasing a home. You may want to request the seller leave the existing appliances, if they were stipulating that these were not included with the sale of the home, as an example.

If you had concerns about the seller leaving something in the house that you did not want, you could include in your offer to have them remove it before you take possession in your offer. Once again, your Realtor is your best resource to help you identify these kinds of issues as they arise, and help you submit the purchase offer that works for you. This is where having an experienced 'buyers agent' on your side really pays off.

DISCLOSURE STATEMENTS

The purchase contract, and requirements for submissions of offers to purchase vary from State to State. There are usually additional forms you are required to sign, that must be submitted with an offer. Some of these include a 'Sellers Disclosure Statement', which is the sellers' detailed disclosure on the condition of the home according to their knowledge. A 'Lead-Based Paint Disclosure', which is a Federal Law covering homes built before 1972, which used lead-based paint as the primary source of paint.

There are also regional disclosures, and State specific disclosure requirements and forms. (For example, parts of Arizona require a buyer to sign a 'Luke Air Force Base Flight Path Disclosure form' getting understanding and agreement that your home is near or within the flight path of the local Air Force base.) Your Realtor will be familiar with the requirements of which forms you will need to sign before the offer is submitted.

Once your offer is submitted, it will be reviewed by the seller and the seller's Realtor. There is usually a time frame indicated in your offer in which they have to respond, or the offer is voided. When they receive it, they will review it. They may wait until the end of the allotted time to respond, or they may respond rapidly and promptly. Once they have gone through the offer, they will do one of three things with it.

1) They will accept it as written.

2) They will counter the offer and include changes, modifications, adjustments, clarifications, etc.

3) They will reject the offer outright, or not respond at all and thereby reject the offer.

If they accept the offer as written, then you are all set to move forward with your home inspections, and perform on the contract. If they make a counter offer, then you will have to review this counter offer with your Realtor and decide whether to accept, counter or reject the new offer.

If they have countered it, you are no longer bound by the original offer, and can walk away from the offer without consequence as it is a new offer to you that you now have the right to accept or not. If they reject the original offer entirely, you can seek to write a new offer or move onto seeking another property if you choose.

Your Realtor can advise you as to whether a counter-offer is within reason, or how proposed changes in the terms of the contract can affect you in the long or short term. Contract law as it relates to the conveyance and sale of property is ever-changing, and your Realtor will be familiar with this as it is their profession. If a counter-offer being proposed is going to ultimately not work for your pre-approved loan program, or create some other known liability for you as a buyer, he/she will be able to direct you as to the best course of action.

A contract negotiation can go back and forth until a mutually acceptable agreement is reached where all parties commit to the contract. Sometimes there can be no agreement reached, and you must know when to move on or reconsider accepting an earlier proposal if you still want the house.

This is where having a Realtor once again is a vital tool and having one represent you in the negotiation can make all the difference between you getting a good deal or not. An experienced Realtor will help you navigate the negotiation process and avoid serious pitfalls, and ultimately help you arrive at your goal.

MULTIPLE OFFER SITUATIONS

In the process of placing an offer on a home, is can happen that you place an offer on a home at the same time one or more other buyers do so as well. Particularly with bank foreclosures, the bank will often go back to all prospective buyers and inform them that there is a 'Multiple Offer Situation' and that they are asking all buyers to come back with their 'highest and best' counter offer on the home. This is where you need to really examine how important it is to you to buy this home. You will want to examine your criteria in a new unit of time to be sure it is what you desire. You will want to consult with your Realtor to get their advice. Sometimes when countering with a multiple offer situation, it is not just about price. It can be about the closing costs, inspections, the loan program you are submitting your offer with, etc.

Banks reviewing an offer will typically give importance to the following in their review:

1) The dollar amount of the offer submitted.

2) Cash offers.

3) Conventional financing offers.

4) Government financing offers.

5) What additional items you are asking the bank to pay for (closing costs, inspections, etc.)

It is not just the price that is often factored in with a bank selling a foreclosure. It is also 'how fast can we close?' Cash offers typically can close in a much fast time frame than a financed offer. A conventional financed offer will often have less stringent requirements than a government loan program. Financing requirements can often require renegotiations on specific repairs required after the appraisal is done, which can cost the seller more money, and create further delays. Fees one is asking for the seller to pay for such as closing costs and inspections will be deducted from their net settlement numbers, and compared to other offers on the table.

It is not unheard of for the above reasons so see a bank take a lower priced cash offer as opposed to a higher priced financed offer. It all has to do with these two factors: *final settlement net value* and *speed of the transaction*. A bank approaching the end of a fiscal year or quarter may be more inclined to take a cash offer for considerably less money if it means that house is no longer on their books at the end of the quarter for example. This can be a benefit for a cash buyer, but a detriment for a financed buyer.

So with this in mind, one seldom is given the information on the competitive offers under consideration in a 'highest and best' multiple offer situation. One can only make the best choice for themselves. If you find you really want the house, you may want to offer more than the listing price in certain circumstances if your Realtor can help you with comparable sales information in the area.

You do not want to offer more that what the home could be appraised for, as this will also work against you as well. So it is a delicate balance of many factors that must be considered in your response. Sometimes it is best to just hold firm with your original offer, and accept what comes, rather than pay too much for what a home is worth.

Once you have an accepted purchase agreement, what is next? Well, let's move on to the next chapter.

Chapter Eight:

MEETING THE COMMITMENTS

Once the purchase contract is accepted, there will be a lot of commitments you will need to accomplish as a buyer, often with strict time restraints. All purchase contracts have time targets to be met. These include funding, inspections, closing dates, etc.

To be late on any of these can mean compromise, penalties, required extensions and/or default on the contract.

So you want to be sure to work as rapidly as

you can and meet all the points on the commitment as stipulated to avoid complications in the process.

Some of the areas you can expect are as follows:

PROVIDING PERSONAL FINANCIAL INFORMATION

Your Loan Officer will often have a list of financial documents they will need for you to gather that will be an integral toward getting the loan approved. This will often include the following (which is by no means a complete list):

- A copy of your social security card.

- A copy of your driver's license or State I.D.

- Bank statements.

- Tax Returns.

- Paycheck stubs.

- Employer contact information and employment history.

- Special applications related to the loan program you are applying for.

- School records (In some cases where work history cannot be proven).

- Proof or records of savings, stocks, bonds, Certificates of Deposit, etc.

- Verification of payment on past items that may still be present on your credit report.

- Government records.

- Legal or court documents, such as divorce decrees, etc.

- Copies of legal trusts, inheritance or estate records.

- Income verification records of all kinds.

- Records of payment history with other creditors.

- Loan origination fees.

- All manner of records or information needed to clarify information for the underwriter.

Find out from your lender specifically what they need. It important to start gathering this data as soon as you can, and get it to your lender in a timely manner so that the loan can be ready so that you can close on the sale of the home as stipulated in the contract. Due to the rise in identity theft in the age of the internet, I recommend that you meet with any lender in person initially, before providing them with your private financial records.

PERFORMING HOME INSPECTIONS

All the inspections your Realtor can help you schedule and arrange. Some of the inspectors may require money up front. Some can be paid as part of the closing settlement. You will often want to be present during or right after the inspections are done, so that you can benefit from the home inspector walking you through the home and getting oriented to its condition. Termite and pest inspections should be included in these actions, and are often a requirement in certain States.

The results of inspection can sometimes result in you not buying the home if the cost of repairs required is too high. Often you can submit an addendum to the contract and negotiate adjustments or modifications to the earlier contract, as a result of information uncovered in the inspection process. Inspections are a vital necessity, so that you can get that third party professional evaluation on the condition of the property you intend to purchase. Be certain to use a reputable inspector, and if your state requires licensing, then be sure he or she is properly licensed.

PRESERVING YOUR CREDIT CONDITION FOR CLOSING

The gravest error a new homebuyer can do during the loan approval process is to go on a shopping spree in preparation for their new home. Until you have closed on the home, hold off or minimize extensive purchases. The reason for this is that it will show up on your credit card statements, or as a reduction in your bank account, and could jeopardize your financial position in the eyes of the underwriter.

I once knew a lady named Sally Johnson that was in the process of buying a new home. She was pre-approved by her lender, after her credit score was pulled. She then provided all the documentation needed for the underwriter, and her loan officer said the loan should be ready to close in three weeks on a Friday. On the Wednesday prior to closing she went shopping for new furniture and purchased a very expensive bedroom set, and arranged for it to be delivered on Friday afternoon. She made the mistake of paying for it on her credit card. On Friday morning prior to the closing, the underwriter requested that her credit report be pulled again as a condition of closing.

The report was pulled by the loan officer, and suddenly this large debt that was not present before was almost blinking off the page into the eyes of the underwriter. As a result the underwriter disapproved the final package and she lost her house.

She also had to return the furniture and paid a sizeable re-stocking fee as a result with the company she bought it from. It took her three more months to get re-qualified for another loan, and by that time the interest rates had gone up and she could not get the same program.

When you are going through a loan approval process, every detail of your financial picture is being examined by the underwriter. The underwriter is the person that is reviewing your file for the approval of the loan behind the scenes. They can request a fresher version of your credit report be pulled, so you do not want dramatic changes to occur on your *debt to income ratio* as a result of increased debt. For example, if you are going to buy new items prior to move in, get the items held on lay-a-way and pay for it right after you close, or in the days following.

HAVING FUNDS AVAILABLE FOR CLOSING

Whenever you purchase a house, you will often be required to bring money for the closing. This can vary depending on the loan program and purchase contract arrangements. It is important to make sure the funds are available for immediate withdrawal prior to closing. These funds must be available in a check or cash form. One cannot use a credit card. Some of the types of fees that are covered in closing costs include the following:

- Property Taxes

- Insurance

- Brokers' fees

- Escrow fees

- Title Insurance Premium

- Deed recording fee

- Title transfer tax

- Appraisal fees

- Miscellaneous administrative fees

If you are required to bring additional funds to closing, always remember that the funds should be made with a bank certified check. Closing fees are one-time costs that must be paid before the loan can be 'closed' or funded.

You will need to consult with your lender or Realtor to verify who the check is to be made out to, but in most cases you will likely be closing at a title company or attorney's office, and it usually made out to the title company or attorney office that is overseeing the closing.

A 'Title Company' is an intermediary company that oversees the legal transaction, and verifies for the lender that all documents are signed and initialed in accordance with their loan program.

Some States such as North Carolina for example, use an attorney to close transactions instead. They also collect all closing fees and taxes, liens, utility bills, etc. are paid that are owned on the property as part of the closing process. They also do a legal search on the property prior to closing, to verify ownership. This is called doing a 'Title Search'.

In doing so they provide an insurance policy that protects you from someone else coming along later and claiming title to the property. Title Companies members of an organization of Title Insurance companies called 'American Land Title Association (ALTA)' which has adopted certain insurance policy forms to standardize coverage on a national basis.

A title insurance policy is a form of coverage that insures a property owner from any other party making or attempting to make a prior claim of ownership or rights to the property after it is sold. This policy also covers the lender and seller should a prior claim arise.

HOMEOWNERS INSURANCE

All mortgages will require that you obtain a

homeowners insurance policy for the new home prior to closing. The stipulations that will be required for the policy should be discussed with your lender. I recommend that you shop for your insurance policy with at least three different sources, to compare rates, because they do vary. You can usually get a name of an insurance agent from your lender, and another one from your Realtor and another from a friend or family member.

This will give you a chance to compare rates, and save yourself some money. Once you have chosen your insurance carrier, ask them to fax in a letter verifying coverage to your lender and/or your title company. This document is a statement from the insurance carrier that you are covered for the home, and it will define the type of coverage.

ESCROW ON TAXES & INSURANCE

When you set up a mortgage, you can decide whether you want the mortgage company to set aside insurance and taxes in a separate account called an 'escrow' account.

This essentially rolls your property taxes and

insurance payment into your monthly mortgage payment, and these bills are paid annually from the escrow account. If you do not have the taxes and insurance payment escrowed, you will receive these bills in the mail separately and you will be responsible for paying them as they come due. The decision to set up an escrow account needs to be made prior to closing, and you will need to notify your lender of your decision on this.

SUMMARIZING THE COMMITMENTS

In summary, when one talks about meeting the commitment as a buyer in purchasing a home, there will be many steps to take between the accepted contract and the actual closing of the home.

Keeping organized, and accomplishing each task in a rapidly as you can accomplish them is the best recipe for a smooth purchasing

experience. Utilize your resources during this period by conferring with your lender and your Realtor.

It is an exciting sense of accomplishment when you finally arrive at the day of closing. This is what we will cover in the next chapter, entitled 'Ending with the keys'.

Chapter Nine:

ENDING WITH THE KEYS

You have finally come to the day of closing after days or weeks of answering questions and providing document after document to your lender. A 'Closing' is where the file on the transaction is brought to finality and closed, and ownership of the property transfers from seller to buyer.

By the time you reach this day, you will have covered a great deal of ground. You will have completed your inspections, and have walked through the property, and should be satisfied with the outcome.

You will have taken all the steps in the prior chapters, the magic day of closing will have arrived. Your journey has led you here.

WHAT HAPPENS AT CLOSING?

When you are buying a home, a closing is typically done at an attorney's office or title office. If can also be done at another location, where the title company representative comes there to oversee the closing.

The representative from the title company is responsible for seeing that the legal requirements are followed for the transfer of property. Some of the basic documents you will be signing are mortgage documents, settlement statements, deed recording documents, tax related documents, and land division forms. The types of forms and documents to sign vary from State to State, and these will all be covered with you at closing by the closing officer.

The Realtor and loan officer you are working with can be very helpful in explaining the various documents you will have to sign, and prepare you for the closing. Having one or both present at your closing can help you catch any errors that might be overlooked by whoever prepared the documents. The bulk of the documents in any closing are typically with the mortgage itself. Each lending institution establishes how they present the mortgage, and some are more comprehensive than others. In any event, you should be prepared to sign several documents at your closing if you have a mortgage.

I could perhaps spend a great deal of time on the subject of your day of closing; however, they will vary from State to State. The paramount idea to remember to arrive at a smooth closing is: preparation.

The most important things to bring to the closing are as follows:

- ➢ You State I.D. or Drivers License

- ➢ Any funds you were told to bring (in certified check form, usually made out to the title company).

- ➢ All parties present that are required to sign documents.

➢ Any other documents your lender or Realtor instructed you to bring that are related to your specific closing. (I.e. Power of Attorney, Insurance documents, etc.)

The fun part about any closing is receiving the keys from the former owner. This typically is symbolic of the process being completed. There are however, a few things you will need to do immediately after a closing. Specifically, making sure the utilities are transferred into your name. You should get the names of the gas, electric, water and waste removal services for the home either from the former owner at closing or your Realtor who will be familiar with the area.

Usually gas, electric and waste removal companies can switch service into your name with a phone call. Often water departments require that you pay them a visit and show proof of ownership. The easiest time to do this is right after your closing, so you can just show them your closing settlement papers.

This is also a time to ask any final questions you may have of the former owners. Prior to this point you most likely will have had limited contact with them as negotiations are often done through your Realtor. This is a good time to learn some things about the home that you may still have questions about.

After the closing is done, you own the home. At this point you can celebrate and enjoy your new home! You will have the keys, and you can get busy with moving in!

There are a few things to keep in mind after you have become a homeowner for the first time, and those will be covered in the next chapter.

Chapter Ten:

EUREKA! HOMEOWNERSHIP!

You made it! Now you have a home of your own!

There are basic common sense points to take into consideration as a new homeowner. Here is a list of 21 points I have collected that you might find to be among the most important. I have divided these points into four different groups: 'Legal Basics', 'Home Care & Maintenance', 'Health & Safety' and 'Neighborly Etiquette'.

LEGAL BASICS

Make sure you switch your utilities into your

name immediately following the closing. This was covered in the last chapter, but it is important to repeat it as this is sometimes forgotten.

Go to the post office and notify them of your new residence.

Send cards to all your friends, creditors and contacts of your new address.

Keep in and maintain your system of organized finances. Keep your mortgage documents in a secure place in your system of records.

Check your credit report regularly at: *www.annualcreditreport.com* or *www.myfico.com*.

Remember to keep a secure record of your passwords, so that you can access your account again without difficulty. I recommend checking your credit report minimally 1-2 times a year.

Review your insurance policy. If you have a mortgage you will have some form of homeowners insurance since it's a condition of obtaining most any mortgage. But is the policy you have enough? In the event of a disaster, you may not have enough insurance to cover the full costs of replacing your home.

Many policies exclude outdoor structures, certain kinds of construction materials and finishes, and the extra living expenses needed while your home is being rebuilt. Find an insurance agent you trust and go over your policy in detail.

Carefully check out the following items: personal property coverage, building replacement costs which change over time, and liability in the event of an accident occurring on your property. File a claim only on major losses. Insurance companies increasingly raise premiums or deny coverage to homeowners that make repeated claims.

Even though you've just bought your home, stay attentive to mortgage rates and deals. Be open to the idea of re-financing if interest rates improve over what you received with your mortgage. Find a mortgage broker you trust and speak to that person four times a year.

There used to be a rule of thumb that if interest rates dropped more than 2% a year it was worth refinancing. In recent years, the variety of mortgage products on the market, including those with zero closing costs, has made refinancing worthwhile even with smaller interest rate fluctuations. Avoid variable rates that adjust in 3 years or less and look for mortgages without prepayment penalties.

Keep good records for your taxes. The government allows you to deduct remodeling expenses on any capital gains after you sell your home. If you deduct remodeling expenses, you must keep a record of your expenses.

It's a good idea to keep cancelled checks or receipts for at least 5 years even after you sell your home in case you're ever audited. The government also allows you to deduct mortgage interest and real estate taxes from your taxable income while you own the home.

Your mortgage company will send you a statement in January of the mortgage interest you paid during the year. Your property tax authority won't send you a statement of taxes paid. You should keep cancelled checks and the statement stub you got with your tax bill as evidence that you paid your property tax. Most property tax is due in two installments, in December and April. If you can afford it, pay the April bill in December since the government allows you to deduct both payments in the current tax year. Sometimes local tax information is available online, so check with your municipality.

HOME CARE & MAINTENANCE

Read any and all manuals related to your appliances and systems, to familiarize yourself with their use.

If there were any warrantees that transferred to you with the home, such as the furnace, appliances, etc. Be sure to send in the required information to the companies with the warrantee.

Work towards improving your home. Treat it like an investment that you want to increase in value for some later date when you may decide to sell it.

If you have an older home, consider getting a Home Warranty. Remember that basic homeowner insurance is generally for fire and flood damage not for normal wear and tear.

The previous owner may have provided you with a one-year warranty for the major systems in your home - air conditioning, heating, plumbing, electrical, roofing and appliances. This was very likely negotiated into the sale of the house. If not, consider purchasing a home warranty if your house is more than 15 years old and still has most of the original systems. Most of the manufacturers' warranties will have expired on a home that old. If you don't want to spend money replacing these systems, a home warranty, typically costing about $500 a year, will pay for the repair or replacement of covered items that wear out.

When it comes to remodeling, don't go overboard. Many people assume that remodeling will always add monetary value to their home. This is sometimes true but more often it isn't. Most remodeling projects will not return dollar for dollar what they cost. The reason: Remodeling doesn't drive the value of your home.

The marketplace for homes does, and this is driven mainly by economic factors such as interest rates, restrictions on new development and the strength of the job market. If you plan to live in your home for many years, you can spend more since the value you get will be the pleasure of living in a place that suits your tastes. But if you plan to live in it for just a few years, think of it as an investment and be judicious. Some things to consider:

➢ Your remodeling dollars should be proportionate to the price you paid for your home. 5% of your home's purchase price for kitchen and bath renovations is a good rule of thumb.

➢ Meet your neighbors and get a sense of how much they've spent on their homes. Don't spend more than the average remodel in your neighborhood.

➢ The age of your house affects the returns you will get on your remodeling dollars. Generally the older the house, the greater the dollar-for-dollar return. If your house is less than 10 years old, it may not make sense to make more than cosmetic changes.

➢ Check the credentials of professionals you hire for your home carefully. Whether you work with contractors, architects or interior designers, you need to find someone you can trust. A good way to start is to get referrals from friends, neighbors or your real estate agent. In some states, building and home improvement contractors need to be licensed. Check with your state or county authority. Make sure the contractor's license and insurance are current, and find out through the state or county whether there have been any judgments against the contractor for shoddy workmanship or fraud. Sometimes this information is available online. Architects and interior designers are less likely to engage in fraud. Architects don't need a license to do minor work. But if you hire one to make structural changes, the work will need approval from a licensed architect. Interior designers generally don't need a license but some have certification from professional associations. Get any proposed job in writing and make payments in stages only for completed work.

➤ Consider updating interior designs and decorating before you move in. Look into landscaping and gardening to improve the exterior grounds. Plan out your seasonal décor, for the holidays. Take advantage of the internet for researching cost effective ways to do this, if you have a computer or order from catalogs to save money. I have a friend that lives on a five acre property in a very rural area of Michigan, and she swears by the value of resources on the internet, especially during the heavy winter months. She claims to have ordered and received delivery on a majority of the items she has used in remodeling her house. So take a little time to see what local suppliers, as well as national companies are offering materials and products that can be reviewed and purchased over the internet.

➢ Go over your inspection report and review suggested maintenance and repairs. You may have bought your home in "as is" condition or the previous owner may not have done all the repairs needed to keep it in good condition. Go back to the appraisal report and review any action items. One of the first things you should do, especially if there's a lot of rain in your area, is fix anything that can cause water damage to your home. For example, make sure the gutters are cleaned out and that there are no leaks. A leaking or overflowing gutter discharging water can damage exterior walls or the foundation, which are costly to repair. Make sure your land is sloped away from the house and that outside drains are working properly.

HEALTH & SAFETY

Your new home should be updated to improve as well as maintain health and safety. Here a few low-cost ideas: Buy a fire extinguisher and make sure everyone in your family knows where it is kept and how to use it. Install fire alarms within a few feet of every bedroom. Consider a water filter for your sink or refrigerator (if it has a water dispenser), especially if you live in an area without municipal water.

Think about installing a CO_2 detector. CO_2 is a colorless, odorless gas which can leak from malfunctioning furnaces, water heaters and stove, and is dangerous to your health. A CO_2 detector can alert you to leaks and help prevent illness or death. Look into having your home tested for Radon, which is another colorless, odorless gas harmful to long term health.

Whenever you buy a new home, it is always a good safety measure to change the keys for all your locks. Even if the former owners were very nice people, you never know who else has a key. So as a common sense measure, change your locks and keys.

Adjust your security to the level of the neighborhood. Your new home should feel secure but you don't want to feel imprisoned. You might be solicited by security companies who want to sell you hardened locks, and alarm and surveillance systems. You may or may not need these things. How do you know? Go to your local police department and ask them what kinds of crime occur in your neighborhood or block, and how often.

Then talk to a security company about installing a system that protects against the most common crimes. There's no reason to put bars on your windows or doors if burglaries are relatively uncommon. In addition, overprotection can make it difficult to exit your home in a fire or other emergency. I once knew a lady that was the only fenced in property on her block, complete with video cameras and intercoms at the gate. She over-did the security to such a degree that her house was burglarized six times after she got the security system when she was not at home, and no other house in the neighborhood had one instance of crime. The local police rationalized that her over-security was an invitation to criminals; because she was advertising she had very expensive things of great value inside her walls.

Develop a cleaning routine. Give yourself tasks to do at regular intervals. This will give your new home a sense of order. A few ideas: Set aside ½ hour each day to do the following: Make beds, pick up clutter, wipe kitchen counters and take out the trash. Set aside a couple of hours each week, say Saturday, to vacuum floors and drapes, dust furniture, pull weeds or mow the lawn.

Clean windows and appliances monthly. Twice a year, shampoo carpets, wax wood floors, check filters in your heating and air conditioning units, and empty out closets and drawers, discarding items you don't need. As you will find as a homeowner, your storage areas seem to fill up over time, so host a garage sale every so often to purge, purge, purge! I know a couple that holds an annual spring garage sale every year, and they use the money towards their summer vacation.

NEIGHBORLY ETIQUETTE

After you move in, if you have not already done so, meet your neighbors. A 'neighborhood' is communities of people living near each other, and you should develop relationships that in the long run are very beneficial and rewarding.

If there are any neighborhood associations, contact them and introduce you. The best advice anyone ever gave me on joining a group is to contribute and bring something to the group, and ultimately you will be rewarded yourself. Neighborhood associations can be very fun. They also can be very effective in protecting a neighborhood on civic issues, so if one does not exist in your new community, you might consider forming one.

There are numerous sources of great

information that you should avail yourself of as a homeowner. There are magazines, books, and workshops often held at home improvement stores. Your local library is also a great resource for books, videos, DVD's and CD's on all forms of home improvement and homeownership.

Once again, the internet is also a great resource with *YouTube*, and home improvement blogs, etc. You can find many more tips from these resources to help you improve and preserve your investment.

The most important point to remember is to enjoy your new life as a homeowner!

Cheers!

Glossary of Common Real Estate Terms

ABSORPTION RATE: Describes the ratio of the number of properties in an area that have been sold against the number available. Usually in report form to show the volatility of a market.

ABSTRACT OF TITLE: A compilation of the recorded documents relating to a parcel of land, from which an attorney may give an opinion as to the condition of the title. This system is still in use in some parts of Wisconsin and in some other states; but more often giving way to the use of the system of title insurance. (See also: *TITLE INSURANCE*)

ACCELERATION CLAUSE: A provision in a mortgage that gives the lender the right to demand *immediate payment* of the outstanding loan balance under certain circumstances. This is usually when the borrower defaults on the loan, but is can also be for other terms defined in the mortgage.

ACCREDITED BUYER REPRESENTATIVE (ABR): A professional designation earned by REALTORS® who take advanced training in Buyer Representation offered by the Real Estate Buyer's Agent Council (REBAC). (See also: *REAL ESTATE BUYERS AGENT COUNCIL*)

ACRE: A measurement of an area of land that totals 43,560 square feet.

ACTUAL AGE: The amount of time that has passed since a building or other structure was built. (See also: *EFFECTIVE AGE*)

AD VALOREM TAX: Taxes assessed by a State, County or Municipality based on the value of the land and improvements.

ADDENDUM: A supplement to any document that contains additional information pertinent to the subject. Appraisers use an addendum to further explain items for which there was inadequate space on the standard appraisal form. Something added; a list or other material added to a document, letter, contractual agreement, escrow instructions, etc. (See also: *AMENDMENT*).

ADJUSTABLE-RATE MORTGAGE (ARM): A type of mortgage where the interest rate varies based on a particular index, normally the prime lending rate. A loan in which the rate of interest is tied to a specific financial index, with both the rate of interest and the monthly payments subject to change at established adjustment intervals of time.

ADJUSTED SALES PRICE: An opinion of a property's sales price, after adjustments have been made to account for differences between it and another comparable property.

ADJUSTED INTERVAL: This defines the period of time between the changes in the interest rate and/or monthly payment as part of an 'adjustable rate' loan. These intervals will vary depending on the lending institution and the type of loan for which application is being made.

AFFORDABILITY ANALYSIS: A calculation used to determine an individual's likelihood of being able to meet the obligations of a mortgage for a particular property. This analysis takes into account the down payment, closing costs and on-going mortgage payments, as well as the individual's financial application.

AGENCY: Any relationship in which one party (agent) acts for or represents another (principal) under the authority of the latter. Agency involving real property should be in writing, such as listings, Buyer brokerage agreements, trusts, powers of attorney, etc.

AGENT: A person who has been appointed to act on behalf of another for a particular transaction.

ALTA (American Land Title Association): An organization composed of title insurance companies which have adopted certain insurance policy forms to standardize coverage on a national basis.

AMENDMENT: A change to alter a part of an agreement without changing the principal idea or essence.

AMENITY: Any feature of a property that increases its value or desirability. These might include natural amenities such as location or proximity to mountains, or man-made amenities like swimming pools, parks or other recreation.

AMORTIZATION: The repayment of a loan through regular periodic payments. A payment breakdown for a debt, broken into installment payments; consisting of both principal and interest over a defined period of time. The origin of the word 'Amortize' derives from the Latin meaning of 'To put to death'. So Amortization ultimately means to extinguish or 'put to death' a debt or loan.

AMORTIZATION SCHEDULE: The breakdown of individual payments throughout the life of an amortized loan, showing both principal contribution and debt service (interest) fees. (See *AMORTIZATION*)

AMORTIZATION TERM: The length of time over which an amortized loan is repaid. Mortgages are commonly amortized over 15 or 30 years. (See *AMORTIZATION*)

ANNUAL PERCENTAGE RATE (APR): The rate of annual interest charged on a loan.

APPLICATION: A form used to apply for a mortgage loan that details a potential borrower's income, debt, savings and other information used to determine credit worthiness. It often requires disclosure of financial information and credit history.

APPLICATION FEE: A fee, often non-refundable, charged by the lender to cover costs of processing an application.

APPRAISAL: A "defensible" and carefully documented opinion of value usually by an appraiser. Most commonly derived using recent sales of comparable properties by a licensed, professional appraiser. A written formal estimation of the 'estimated current value' of a home.

APPRAISAL REPORT: The end result of the appraisal process, usually consists of one major, standardized form such as the Uniform Residential Appraisal Report form 1004, as well as all supporting documentation and additional detail information. The purpose of the report is to convey the opinion of value of the subject property and support that opinion with corroborating information.

APPRAISED VALUE: An opinion of the fair

market value of a property (as determined by a licensed certified appraiser), following accepted appraisal principals.

APPRAISER: An educated, certified professional with extensive knowledge of real estate markets, values and practices. The appraiser is often the only independent voice in any real estate transaction with no vested interest in the ultimate value or sales price of the property.

APPRECIATION: The natural rise or increase in property value due to market forces.

APR (Annual Percentage Rate): The cost of credit expressed as a yearly rate. It takes into account interest, points and loan origination fee. Since all lenders are required to use the same guidelines in determining APR, this is a good basis for comparing the cost of various loan programs.

ARMS LENGTH TRANSACTION: Any transaction in which the two parties are unconnected and have no overt common interests. Such a transaction most often reflects the true market value of a property.

ASSESSED VALUE: This is a value assigned to

real estate, for taxable purposes, by a local jurisdictional tax assessor.

ASSESSMENT: The function of assigning a value to a property for the purpose of levying taxes.

ASSESSMENT RATIO: The comparative relationship of a property's assessed value to market value.

ASSESSMENTS: (1) The estimating of value of property for tax purposes. (2) A levy against property in addition to general taxes. It can be for improvements such as streets, sewers, etc. (3) Charges against unit owners in a condominium by a condo or homeowners association.

ASSESSOR: The jurisdictional official who performs the assessment and assigns the value of a property.

ASSET: Any item of value which a person owns that is considered appreciating in value.

AUTOMATED UNDERWRITING SYSTEM (AUS): This is a computer program that allows a loan officer to enter a potential borrower's information into it from a submitted application and then reviews it. It provides an instant response as to whether the person will qualify for a loan and for which programs. It is considered to be a rapid and impartial system for preliminarily evaluating an applicant's qualification for a loan.

BALLOON MORTGAGE (OR BALLOON NOTE): A mortgage loan in which the monthly payments are not large enough to repay the loan by the end of the term. So at the end of the term, the remaining balance comes due in a single large payment.

BALLOON PAYMENT: This is the final large payment at the end of a mortgage term.

BANKRUPTCY: When a person or business is unable to pay their debts and seeks protection of the state against creditors. Bankruptcies remain on credit records for up to ten years and can prevent a person from being able to get a loan.

BENEFICIARY: A person or entity named to receive the income or property held in a trust. (See TRUST)

BILL OF SALE: A receipt indicating the sale of property. This is a written document that serves as a record, as when one transfers ownership of personal property.

BORROWER: Anyone who borrows money from a lending source.

BREACH (also called Default): Failure to comply with the terms of a contract.

BROKER (REAL ESTATE): An individual who facilitates the purchase of property by bringing together a buyer and a seller. One who engages in any of several sorts of business activities relating to the financing, rental or sale of real property or a business.

BUNGALOW: A one-story, home-style dating from the early twentieth century. This is often characterized by a low-pitched roof.

BUYER'S AGENT (REPRESENTATIVE): A Real Estate Agent that has a contractual relationship to represent a buyer in a real estate transaction.

CAPE COD COLONIAL: A single-story house style made popular in New England. This is often characterized by a steep roof with gables.

CAVEAT EMPTOR: Literally translated from

Latin: *"Let the buyer beware."* A common business tenet, where it describes the buyer's responsibility for verifying any and all claims, made by the seller of the property. The buyer assumes all risk in their purchase.

CERTIFICATE OF ELIGIBILITY: A document issued by the Veterans Administration that certifies eligibility for a VA loan.

CERTIFICATE OF TITLE: A document designating the legal owner of a parcel of real estate. This is usually provided by a title or abstract of title company. (See also: *TITLE* and *ABSTRACT OF TITLE*)

CERTIFIED RESIDENTIAL SPECIALIST (CRS): A professional designation program offered to REALTORS® that requires over 70 hours of advanced training, and the sale of 25 homes to achieve. The CRS designation is offered only by the Council of Residential Specialists. (See also: *COUNCIL OF RESIDENTIAL SPECIALISTS*)

CHAIN OF TITLE: The complete history of ownership of a piece of property.

CHARGE-OFFS: Any time a creditor has closed

an account and marked the account off as a loss. A designation on a credit report that an account went delinquent, and the closed the account and took it as a loss as opposed to sending it to collections.

CLEAR TITLE: Ownership of property that is not encumbered by any counter-claim or lien.

CLOSING: The process whereby the sale of a property is consummated with the buyer completing all applicable documentation, including signing the mortgage obligation and paying all appropriate costs associated with the sale (See *CLOSING COSTS*). In real estate sales, the procedure in which documents are executed and delivered in return for the payment of the sales price, and the sale (or loan) is completed.

CLOSING COSTS: Describes all appropriate costs generated by the sale of property, which the parties must pay, to complete the transaction. Costs may include appraisal fees, origination fees, title insurance, taxes and any points negotiated in the deal. One-time costs that must be paid before the loan can be "closed" or funded. These costs may include such things as property taxes, insurance, broker's fees, escrow fees, title insurance premium, deed recording fee, title insurance premium, title transfer tax, etc. Escrow instructions will stipulate which portions of the fees are to be paid by Buyer or Seller. An estimate of closing costs will be given to Buyer by the lender within a few days after receiving the loan application. (All or a portion of the closing costs may be financed depending on the loan program.)

CLOSING STATEMENT: The document detailing the final financial arrangement, complete with settlement figures, between a buyer and seller and the costs paid by each.

CO-BORROWER: A second person sharing obligation on the loan and title on the property.

COLLATERAL: An asset which is placed at risk to secure the repayment of a loan.

COLLECTION: The process a lender takes to pursue a borrower who is delinquent on his payments in order to bring the mortgage current again. This includes documentation that may be used in the foreclosure process.

COMMISSION: Compensation earned by a Real Estate Agent for negotiating a purchase or sale of property or otherwise complying with his agency contract.

COMMON AREA ASSESSMENTS: Fees which are charged to the tenets or owners of properties to cover the costs of maintaining areas shared with other tenets or owners. Commonly found in condominium, PUD or office spaces.

COMMON AREAS: Any areas, such as entryways, foyers, pools, recreational facilities or the like, which are shared by the tenets or owners of property nearby. Commonly found in condominium or office spaces.

COMPARABLES: An abbreviated term used by appraisers to describe properties which are similar in size, condition, location and amenities to a subject property whose value is being determined. The Uniform Standards of Professional Appraisal Practice (USPAP) establish clear guidelines for determining a comparable property.

COMPOUND INTEREST: Interest paid on the principal amount, as well as any accumulated interest.

CONCESSIONS: Additional value granted by a

buyer or seller to entice another party to complete a deal.

CONDOMINIUM: A development where individual units are owned, but common areas and amenities are shared equally by all owners.

CONSTRUCTION LOAN: A loan made to a builder or home owner that finances the initial construction of a property, but is replaced by a traditional mortgage one the property is completed.

CONTINGENCY: Something that must occur before something else happens. Often used in real estate sales when a buyer must sell a current home before purchasing a new one. Or, when a buyer makes an offer that requires a complete home inspection before it becomes official.

CONTRACT: A legally binding agreement, oral or written, between two parties.

CONVENTIONAL MORTGAGE: A traditional, real estate financing mechanism that is not backed by any government or other agency (FHA, VA, etc.).

CONVERTIBLE ARM: A mortgage that begins

and is adjustable, that allows the borrower to convert the loan to a fixed rate within a specific timeframe.

CONVEYANCE: Transfer of title to land. Includes most instruments by which interest in real estate is created, mortgaged or assigned.

COST OF FUNDS INDEX (COFI): An index of financial institutions costs used to set interest rates for some Adjustable Rate Mortgages.

COUNCIL OF RESIDENTIAL SPECIALISTS (CRS): A national organization based in Chicago, Illinois that provides advanced training for REALTORS®. The Council of Residential Specialists offers a special designation for REALTORS® called 'Certified Residential Specialist (CRS)' which is earned after over 70 hours of advanced training, and a minimum of 25 homes sold. CRS is affiliated and endorsed by the National Association of REALTORS®. Less than 4% of REALTORS® nationally earn the CRS designation.

COVENANT: A stipulation in any mortgage that, if not met, can be cause for the lender to foreclose.

CREDIT: A loan of money for the purchase of property, real or personal. Credit is either secured by an asset, such as a home, or unsecured.

CREDIT HISTORY: A record of debt and payments on such, past and present. Used by mortgage lenders in determining credit worthiness of individuals.

CREDITOR: A person to whom money is owed.

CREDIT REPORT: A detailed report of an individual's past credit performance, employment and the history of where they have lived. It is prepared by a credit bureau. Used by lenders to determine credit worthiness of individuals.

CREDIT REPOSITORY: Large companies that gather and store financial and credit information about individuals who apply for credit.

CUL-DE-SAC: A dead-end street with only one entrance/exit. Such a street is usually characterized by a circular turn-a-round at the end.

DEBT: An obligation to repay some amount owed. This may or may not be monetary.

DEBT EQUITY RATIO: The ratio of the amount a mortgagor still owes on a property to the amount of equity they have in the home. Equity is calculated at the fair-market value of the home, less any outstanding mortgage debt.

DEED: A document indicating the ownership of a property.

DEED OF TRUST: A document which transfers title in a property to a trustee, whose obligations and powers are stipulated. Often used in mortgage transactions. An instrument used in many states in place of a mortgage. Property is transferred to a trustee by the borrower (trustor), in favor of the lender (beneficiary), and re-conveyed upon payment in full.

DEED OF RECONVEYANCE: A document which transfers ownership of a property from a Trustee back to a borrower who has fulfilled the obligations of a mortgage.

DEFAULT: The condition in which a borrower has failed to meet the obligations of a loan or mortgage.

DELINQUENCY: The state in which a

borrower has failed to meet payment obligations on time.

DEPOSIT: Cash given along with an offer to purchase property, also called earnest money. (See *EARNEST DEPOSIT)*

DEPRECIATION: The natural decline in property value due to market forces or depletion of resources.

DETACHED SINGLE-FAMILY HOME: A single building improvement intended to serve as a home for one family.

DISCOUNT POINTS: Points paid in addition to the loan origination fee to get a lower interest rate. One point is equal to one percent of the loan amount.

DUE-ON-SALE CLAUSE: A clause in a mortgage giving the lender the right to demand payment of the full balance when the borrower sells the property.

DUPLEX: A single-building improvement which is divided and provides two units which serve as homes to two families.

DWELLING: A house or other building which serves as a home.

DOWN PAYMENT: An amount paid in cash for a property, with the intent to mortgage the remaining amount due.

EARNEST MONEY DEPOSIT: A cash deposit made to a home seller to secure an offer to buy the property. This amount is often forfeited if the buyer decides to withdraw his offer. It shows good faith that the transaction proposal will be honored.

EASEMENT: The right of a non-owner of property to exert control over a portion or all of a property. For example, power companies often own an easement over residential properties for access to their power lines, or two properties adjacent to each other might share a common driveway.

ECONOMIC DEPRECIATION: The decline in property value caused by external forces, such as neighborhood blight or adverse development.

EFFECTIVE AGE: The subjective, estimated age of a property based on its condition, rather than the actual time since it was built. Excessive wear and tear can cause a property's effective age to be greater than its actual age.

EMINENT DOMAIN: The legal process whereby a government can take ownership of a piece of property in order to convert it to public use. Often, the property owner is paid fair-market value for the property.

ENCROACHMENT: A building or other improvement on one property which invades another property or restricts its usage.

ENCUMBRANCE: A claim against a property. Examples are mortgages, liens and easements. A claim, lien, charge, or liability attached to and binding real property. Any 'right to' or 'interest in', land which may exist in one other than the owner, but which will not prevent the transfer of fee title.

EQUAL CREDIT OPPORTUNITY ACT (ECOA): U.S. federal law requiring that lenders afford people equal chance of getting credit without discrimination based on race, religion, age, sex etc.

EQUITY: The difference between the fair market value of a property and that amount an owner owes on any mortgages or loans secured by the property.

EQUITY BUILD-UP: The natural increase in the amount of equity an owner has in a property, accumulated through market appreciation and debt repayment.

ESCROW: An amount retained by a third party in a trust to meet a future obligation. Often used in the payment of annual taxes or insurance for real property.

ESCROW ACCOUNT: An account setup by a mortgage servicing company to hold funds with which to pay expenses such as: homeowners insurance and property taxes.

ESCROW AGENT: A neutral third party, appointed to act as custodian for documents and funds.

ESCROW ANALYSIS: An analysis performed by the lender (usually once each year), to see that the amount of money going into the escrow account each month is correct for the forecasted expenses.

ESCROW DISBURSEMENTS: The payout of

funds from an escrow account to pay property expenses: such as taxes and insurance.

ESTATE: The total of all property and assets owned by an individual.

ESTOPPELS: The prevention of one from asserting a legal right because of prior actions inconsistent with its assertion.

EXAMINATION OF TITLE: The report on the title of a property from the public records or an abstract of the title. (See also: *TITLE COMPANY* and *ABSTRACT OF TITLE)*

EXCLUSIVE LISTING: An agreement between the owner of a property and a real estate agent giving the agent exclusive right to sell the property.

EXECUTOR: The person named in a will to administer the estate.

FAÇADE: The front exposure of any building. This is often used to describe an artificial or false front which is not consistent with the construction of the rest of the building.

FAIR CREDIT REPORTING ACT: Federal laws, regulating the way credit agencies disclose consumer credit reports. It defines the remedies available to consumers for disputing and correcting mistakes on their credit history.

FAIR HOUSING: This refers to Federal and State laws that embrace the ideal of equal housing opportunities for everyone. *Fair Housing laws* prohibits anyone in the profession of real estate, or mortgage lending from refusing to negotiate for or engage in a real estate transaction with a person because of race, color, religion, national origin, age, sex, familial status, marital status, or mental and physical handicap. In some states, this list is further expanded to include height, weight, sexual orientation and HIV Positive. Discrimination in the terms of a rental, lease, or purchase is against the law. It also includes in the furnishing of facilities in connection with such as a transaction, such as appraising a home, property inspections, land surveys, etc. This also extends to publishing or advertising, directly or indirectly, or intent to make a limitation, specification or discrimination based on any of the categories listed above. The origin of these civil rights goes back to the Civil Rights Act of 1866. It was later expanded with the Civil Rights Act of 1968, and the later the 'Persons with

Disabilities Civil Rights Act' of 1976. Many states have followed with their own civil rights acts pertaining to each state constitution.

FAIR MARKET VALUE: The price at which two unrelated parties, under no duress, are willing to transact business. Amount of money for which property will sell following negotiations between the owner of such property who will sell but is not required to sell and a proposed Buyer for such property who is not obligated to buy such property.

FANNIE MAE: A private, shareholder-owned company that works to make sure mortgage money is available for people to purchase homes. Created by Congress in 1938, Fannie Mae is the nation's largest source of financing for home mortgages.

FEDERAL DEPOSIT INSURANCE CORPORATION (FDIC): The U.S. Government agency created in 1933 which maintains the stability of and public confidence in the nation's financial system by insuring deposits and promoting safe and sound banking practices.

FEDERAL HOUSING ADMINISTRATION (FHA): A sub-agency of the U.S. Department of Housing and Urban Development created in the 1930's to facilitate the purchase of homes by low-income, first-time home buyers. It currently provides federally-subsidized mortgage insurance for private lenders.

FHA MORTGAGE: A mortgage that is insured by the Federal Housing Administration (FHA).

FICO: 'FICO' is an acronym for 'Fair, Isaac and Company'. Fair, Isaac & Co. developed the credit scoring system that is used today by the three major credit bureaus: *Experian, TransUnion* and *Equifax*.

FIRST MORTGAGE: The description of the primary loan or mortgage secured by a piece of property.

FIXED-RATE MORTGAGE (FRM): A mortgage which has a fixed rate of interest over the life of the loan.

FIXTURE: Any piece of personal property which becomes permanently affixed to a piece of real property. It generally refers to property that it attached to the home, such as light fixtures, toilets, counter tops, etc.

FLOOD INSURANCE: This describes supplemental insurance which covers a home owner for any loss due to water damage from a flood. This is often required by lenders for homes located in federally designated flood zones.

FLOODPLAIN: The extent of the land adjoining water which, because of its topography, would flood if the water overflowed its banks.

FLOOR PLAN: The representation of a building which shows the basic outline of the structure, as well as detailed information about the positioning of rooms, hallways, doors, stairs and other features. Often includes detailed information about other fixtures and amenities.

FORECLOSURE: The process whereby a lender can claim the property used by a borrower to secure a mortgage and sell the property to meet the obligations of the loan.

FORFEITURE: The loss of property or money due to the failure to meet the obligations of a mortgage or loan secured by that property.

FUNCTIONAL OBSOLESCENCE: A decrease in the value of property due to a feature or lack thereof which renders the property undesirable. Functional obsolescence can also occur when the surrounding area changes, rendering the property unusable for it's originally intended purpose.

GENERAL LIEN: A broad-based claim against several properties owned by a defaulting party.

GOVERNMENT MORTGAGE: Any mortgage insured by a government agency, such as the FHA or VA.

GRANTEE: Any person who is given ownership of a piece of property by another party or entity.

GRANTOR: Any person who gives away ownership of a piece of property.

HAZARD INSURANCE: This is insurance covering damage to a property caused by hazards such as fire, wind and accident.

HAZARDOUS MATERIALS: Substances that may be hazardous to health (i.e., asbestos, radon gas, lead based paint).

HOME EQUITY LINE OF CREDIT (HELOC): A type of mortgage loan that allows the borrower to draw cash against the equity in his home.

HOME INSPECTION: A complete examination of a building to determine its structural integrity and uncover any defects in materials or workmanship which may adversely affect the property or decrease its value.

HOME INSPECTOR: A person who performs professional home inspections. This is usually a professional with an extensive knowledge of houses and their construction methods. Their knowledge will also include common house problems, how to identify those problems and how to correct them.

HOMEOWNER'S ASSOCIATION: An organization of home owners in a particular neighborhood or development formed to facilitate the maintenance of common areas and to enforce any building restrictions or covenants.

HOMEOWNER'S INSURANCE: A policy which covers a home owner for any loss of property due to accident, intrusion or hazard.

HOMEOWNER'S WARRANTY: An insurance policy covering the repair of systems and appliances within the home for the coverage period.

HUD-1 SETTLEMENT STATEMENT: A standardized, itemized list, published by the U.S. Department of Housing and Urban Development (HUD), of all anticipated CLOSING COSTS connected with a particular property purchase.

IMPROVEMENTS: Any item added to vacant land with the intent of increasing its value or usability.

INCOME PROPERTY: A piece of property whose highest and best use is the generation of income through rents or other sources.

INDEMNIFY: To make payment for a loss.

INDEPENDENT APPRAISAL: An estimation of value created by a professional, certified appraiser with no vested interest in the value of the property.

INDEX: Used by lenders to calculate the interest adjustments on adjustable rate loans. Some indexes are more volatile than others; this can affect adjustments in the interest rate and, subsequently, the monthly payment. Because these indexes reflect the general movement of interest rates, they tend to keep the rate on an adjustable rate loan in line with market conditions.

INITIAL RATE: An interest rate charged for the first six or twelve months of an adjustable rate loan. Normally this rate will be lower than prevailing fixed market rates.

INSPECTION: The examination of a piece of property, its buildings or other amenities.

INSTALLMENT LOAN: A line of credit for a fixed sum, with pre-set monthly payments including principle and interest. Example: loans for vehicles or equipment.

INSURABLE TITLE: The title to property which has been sufficiently reviewed by a title insurance company, such that they are willing to insure it as free and clear.

INTEREST RATE: A percentage of a loan or mortgage value that is paid to the lender as compensation for loaning funds.

INTEREST RATE CAP: A safeguard built into an adjustable rate loan to protect the consumer against dramatic increases in the rate of interest and, consequently, in the monthly payment. For example, an adjustable rate loan may have a two percentage point limit per year on the amount of increase or decrease, as well as a five percentage point limit (increase or decrease) over the life of the loan.

INTERIM FINANCING: Temporary financing usually for construction or bridge loans to facilitate the purchase of a new home before the sale of the previous home has been closed.

INVESTMENT PROPERTY: Any piece of property that is expected to generate a financial return. This may come as the result of periodic rents or through appreciation of the property value over time.

JOINT TENANCY: A situation where two or more parties own a piece of property together. Each of the owners has an equal share, and may not dispose of or alter that share without the consent of the other owners.

JUDGMENT: An official court decision. If the judgment requires payment from one party to another, the court may put a lien against the payees property as collateral.

JUDICIAL FORECLOSURE: A type of foreclosure conducted as a civil suit in a court of law.

JUNIOR MORTGAGE: A mortgage, such as a second mortgage, which is subordinate as security to another mortgage.

LAND CONTRACT: Describes an installment contract for the sale of land. The Seller (vendor) has legal title until paid in full. The Buyer (vendee) has equitable title during the contract term. See the Author's popular books: '*Understanding Land Contract Homes: In Pursuit of the American Dream*' and '*Land Contract Homes for Investors*' for further study.

LATE CHARGE: An extra charge, or penalty added to a regular mortgage payment when the payment is made late by an amount of time specified in the original loan document.

LATENT DEFECTS: Any defect in a piece of property which is not readily apparent, but which has an impact of the value. Structural damage or termite infestation would be examples of latent defects.

LEASE: A contract between a property owner and a tenant specifying the payment amount, terms and conditions, as well as the length of time the contract will be in force.

LEASE OPTION: A lease agreement that gives the tenant an option to buy the property. Usually, a portion of the regular monthly rent payment will be applied towards the down payment.

LEGAL DESCRIPTION: The description of a piece of property, identifying its specific location in terms established by the municipality or other jurisdiction in which the property resides. This is often related in specific distances from a known landmark or intersection.

LEGAL NOTICE: The notice required by law in a particular case. It may be actual notice, constructive notice, etc.

LENDER: In real estate, the person or entity who loans funds to a buyer. In return, the lender will receive periodic payments, including principal and interest amounts.   It can also be any person or organization that loans money to a borrower.

LENGTH OF CREDIT HISTORY: The length of time a borrower has had established credit accounts that are reported on his/her credit report.

LIABILITIES: A person's outstanding debt obligations.

LIABILITY INSURANCE: Insurance that covers against potential lawsuit brought against a property owner for alleged negligence resulting in damage to another party.

LIEN: Any claim against a piece of property resulting from a debt or other obligation.

LISTING AGENT: The term for a Real Estate agent that has an 'exclusive right to sell' contract with a seller to sell their home. The home is considered to be 'listed' for sale through a Real Estate agent.

LOAN: Money borrowed, to be repaid with interest, according to the specific terms and conditions of the loan.

LOAN OFFICER: A person that "sells" loans, representing the lender to the borrower, and the borrower to the lender.

LOAN ORIGINATION: How a lender refers to the process of writing new loans.

LOAN SERVICING: The processing of

payments, mailing of monthly statements, management and disbursement of escrow funds, etc. Typically carried out by the loan company you make payments to.

LOAN-TO-VALUE RATIO (LTV): The comparison of the amount owed on a mortgaged property to its fair market value.

LOCK-IN: An agreement between a lender and a borrower, guaranteeing an interest rate for a loan if the loan is closed within a certain amount of time.

LOCK-IN PERIOD: The amount of time the lender has guaranteed an interest rate to a borrower.

MANUFACTURED HOUSING: Once known as "mobile homes," manufactured housing is any building which has been constructed off site, then moved onto a piece of real property.

MATURITY: The date on which the principal balance of a financial instrument becomes due and payable.

MERGED CREDIT REPORT: A credit report

derived from data obtained from multiple credit agencies. This usually is contains information from all three credit bureaus in a single report.

METES AND BOUNDS: A traditional way of describing property, generally expressed in terms of distance from a known landmark or intersection, and then following the boundaries of the property back to its origin.

MILL RATE: A percentage applied to the assessed valuation to determine taxes.

MORTGAGE: A financial arrangement wherein an individual borrows money to purchase real property and secures the loan with the property as collateral.

MORTGAGE BANKER: This describes a financial institution that provides primary and secondary mortgages to home buyers.

MORTGAGE BROKER: This is a person or organization that serves as a middleman to facilitate the mortgage process. Brokers often represent multiple mortgage bankers and offer the most appropriate deal to each buyer.

MORTGAGEE: The entity that lends money in a real estate transaction.

MORTGAGE INSURANCE: This describes a policy that fulfills the obligations of a mortgage when the policy holder defaults, or is no longer able to make payments. The policy protects the mortgage lender.

MORTGAGE INSURANCE PREMIUM (MIP): A fee that is often included in mortgage payments that pays for mortgage insurance coverage.

MORTGAGE LIFE INSURANCE: A policy that fulfills the obligations of a mortgage when the policy holder dies.

MORTGAGE NOTE: A promissory note secured by a mortgage and executed by mortgagor at the same time as the mortgage for the amount stated in the mortgage, with the legal description of land described in the mortgage also stated in such note.

MORTGAGOR: The entity that borrows money in a real estate transaction.

NEIGHBORHOOD: 1) A community, district or

area especially with regards to some point of reference. 2) The people living near and around a community.

NOTE: A legal document that obligates a borrower to repay a mortgage loan at a stated interest rate during a specified period of time.

NOTICE OF DEFAULT: Formal written notice from a lender to a borrower that default has occurred.

OCCUPANCY: A physical presence within and control of a property.

OLD TERMITE ACTIVITY: Where no termites are currently active, but indications of past activity can be seen.

OPEN ACCOUNTS: Credit accounts that are open and still in use by a borrower. Accounts considered active and in use by the creditor.

OWNER OCCUPIED: The state of property wherein the owner occupies at least some portion of the property.

PAYMENT HISTORY: The running record of a borrowers' performance on paying back borrowed funds.

PERSONAL PROPERTY: Owned items which are not permanently affixed to the land.

PERSONAL OR 'PRINCIPLE' RESIDENCE: The primary domicile where a person or family lives.

PITI: Refers to 'principal', 'interest', 'taxes', and 'insurance'. This describes the complete monthly home loan payment, inclusive of taxes and insurance.

PLAT: A plan or chart of a piece of land which lays out existing or planned streets, lots or other improvements.

POINT: A percentage of a mortgage amount (one point = 1 percent).

POINTS AND FEES: A point is a charge equal to one percent of the principal amount of the loan (e.g., 2 points charged on a $100,000 loan would> equal $2,000). Points are generally payable at closing and may be paid by the Buyer or Seller, or split between them. In addition, a flat dollar amount fee may also be charged. Under some lending programs, a buyer may be allowed to include these points and fees as part of the total amount financed.

PRE-APPROVAL: The process of applying for a mortgage loan and becoming approved for a certain amount at a certain interest rate before a property has been chosen. Pre-approval allows the borrower greater freedom in negotiations with sellers. It does not mean they have been fully approved for a loan, but just states they have met the preliminary lending requirements and been told so by a lender.

PREPAYMENT: Payment made that reduces the principal balance of a loan before the due date and before the loan has become fully amortized.

PREPAYMENT CLAUSE: Clause in mortgage, mortgage note or land contract providing that debtor may pay more than agreed installment payment at any time.

PREPAYMENT PENALTY: A fee that may be charged to a borrower who pays off a loan before it is due.

PRE-QUALIFICATION: Less formal that pre-approval, pre-qualification usually means a written statement from a loan officer indicating his or her opinion that the borrower will be able to become approved for a mortgage loan.

PRIME RATE: The interest rate that a bank and other lending institutions charge other banks or preferred customers.

PRINCIPAL: The amount owed on a mortgage which does not include interest or other fees.

PRINCIPAL BALANCE: The outstanding balance of principal on a mortgage. This does not include the amount of total interest due.

PRIVATE MORTGAGE INSURANCE (PMI): A form of mortgage insurance provided by private, non-government entities. This is normally required when the loan to value ratio is less that 20%. The premium is paid by the borrower and is included in the mortgage payment. (See also: *LOAN TO VALUE RATIO*)

PROCESSING (TURNAROUND) TIME: The amount of time required from the day loan application documents are submitted in full to the day the loan closes and loan funds are disbursed. This is the total processing time for a home loan.

PROPERTY: Any item which is owned or possessed.

PRO-RATE: To allocate between Seller and Buyer their proportionate share of an obligation paid or due.

PUBLIC RECORDS: Any record recorded by a County or State. These can include judicial records, bankruptcies, foreclosures, deeds, etc.

PURCHASE AGREEMENT: A written contract signed by the buyer and seller stating the terms and conditions under which a property will be sold.

QUIT-CLAIM DEED: A legal document which transfers any ownership an individual has in a piece of property. Often used when the amount of ownership is not known or is unclear.

RANCH HOUSE: An architectural style typified by a single-story, low-roof construction popular in the western U.S.

RATE LOCK (OR GUARANTEE): A guarantee from a lender of a specific interest rate for a period of time.

REAL ESTATE: A piece of land and any

improvements or fixtures located on that land.

REAL ESTATE AGENT: A licensed professional who facilitates the buying and selling of real estate.

REAL ESTATE BUYERS AGENT COUNCIL (REBAC): A national organization that offers a special designation for REALTORS® on Buyer Representation in real estate transactions. To earn the designation requires approximately 40 hours of training, in addition to participating in at least 5 transactions as a Buyers Representative. The designation offered by REBAC is entitled 'Accredited Buyer Representative (ABR)' (See also: *ACCREDITED BUYER REPRESENTATIVE*)

REAL ESTATE SETTLEMENT PROCEDURES ACT (RESPA): A federal law requiring lenders to give full disclosure of closing costs to borrowers.

REAL PROPERTY: Land, improvements and appurtenances, and the interest and benefits thereof.

REALTOR®: A designation given to a real estate licensee who is a member of a board associated with the National Association of REALTORS®.

RECORDER: A local government employee whose role it is to keep records of all real estate transactions within the jurisdiction.

RECORDING: The filing of a real estate transaction with the appropriate government agent. A real estate transaction is considered final when it is recorded. (See *RECORDER*)

REMAINING BALANCE: The amount of principal, interest and other costs that have not yet been repaid.

RESIDENTIAL PROPERTY: A piece of property whose highest and best use is the maintenance of a residence.

REVOLVING CREDIT: A type of credit that allows the borrower to make charges against a predetermined line of credit. The customer then pays monthly installments on the amount borrowed, plus interest. Example: Credit Cards are considered revolving lines of credit.

RURAL: An area outside of an established urban area or metropolitan district.

SALE PRICE: The actual price a property sells

for, exclusive of any special financing concessions.

SECOND MORTGAGE: A loan secured by the equity in a home, when a primary mortgage already exists.

SECURED LOAN: This is a loan that is backed by collateral. In the case of a mortgage loan, the collateral is the house.

SEPTIC INSPECTION: An inspection of the septic system of a given property. Sometimes this is a required inspection for closing in a contract.

SERVICING: Mortgage bankers typically retain the right to collect monthly payments and take care of any customer problems. They send a payment to the investor each month. For this service, the mortgage banker receives a small fee (1/4% to 1/2% of the mortgage amount).

SINGLE-FAMILY PROPERTY: A property designed and built to support the habitation of one family.

SUBDIVISION: A residential development that is created from a piece of land which has been subdivided into individual lots.

SUBJECT PROPERTY: This is a term which indicates a property which is being appraised.

SURVEY: A specific map of a piece of property which includes the legal boundaries and any improvements or features of the land. Surveys also depict any rights-of-way, encroachments or easements.

SWEAT EQUITY: The method whereby a home owner develops equity in a property, either during the purchase or throughout its life, by personally constructing improvements rather than paying to have them built.

TERM: The number of years before a loan is scheduled to be paid off. 15-year and 30-year terms are most common.

TERMITE LETTER: An official letter from a certified pest inspection company. The letter states that a property has been inspected and found to have been treated, or free and clear of termite infestation. Some States require such a letter for all real estate closings before transfer of title can occur.

TITLE: A specific document which serves as

proof of ownership.

TITLE COMPANY: An organization which researches and certifies ownership of real estate before it is bought or sold. Title companies also act at the facilitator ensures all parties are paid during the real estate transaction.

TITLE INSURANCE: A policy which insures a property owner should a prior claim arise against the property after the purchase has been completed. This also covers a lender should a question of ownership arise.

TITLE SEARCH: The process whereby the Title Company researches a properties title history and ensures that no outstanding claims exist.

TRANSFER OF OWNERSHIP: Any means by which the ownership of a property changes hands.

TRANSFER OF TAX: Taxes payable when title passes from one owner to another.

TRANSFER TAX OR TRANSFER FEE: A tax on the transfer of real property. Generally based on value of property being transferred (i.e., purchase price). Check statutes for each state. This is also called 'Documentary Transfer Tax' in some States.

TRUST: A legal entity created by a 'Trustor' to place an estate or property in the care of another called a 'Trustee'. A Trustee oversees the responsibility to manage a Trust for the benefit of the 'Beneficiary', who is the party that will receive the estate or property if the Trust is dissolved.

TRUSTEE: A fiduciary who holds or controls property for the benefit of another.

TRUSTOR: A person who creates a Trust. (See *TRUST*)

TRUTH IN LENDING: A federal law requiring full disclosure by lenders to borrowers of all terms, conditions and costs of a mortgage.

TUDOR: A style of architecture typified by exposed stone, wood and brick construction. This is similar in style to English manor homes.

UNDERLYING FINANCING: A mortgage, deed of trust, land contract etc. Prior to (underlying) a land contract, mortgage, etc. on the same property.

UNDERWRITER: This is a person who works for a lending or some other financial company, and oversees the process of a loan, and makes sure a borrower who is applying complies and conforms to the guidelines as defined by the institution they work for. They often have final approval or disapproval authority on any application.

UNENCUMBERED PROPERTY: Any property which has no outstanding claims or liens against it.

USURY: Charging more than the legal rate of interest for the use of money.

VA GUARANTEE MORTGAGE: A mortgage that is guaranteed by the Department of Veterans Affairs (VA).

VETERANS AFFAIRS, DEPARTMENT OF (VA): The successor to the Veteran's Administration, this government agency is responsible for ensuring the rights and welfare of our nation's veterans and their dependents. Among other duties, the VA insures home loans made to veterans.

VESTING: Name(s) in which title property is held.

WALK-THROUGH INSPECTION: A process whereby an appraiser examines a property in preparation for estimating its value. Also, the process of inspecting a property for any damage prior to that property being bought or sold. Sometimes called a 'final walk-through' when buyers do a final review or tour of a home prior to closing.

WARRANTY: An affidavit given to stipulate the condition of a property. The person giving the warranty assumes liability if the condition turns out to be untrue.

WARRANTY DEED: This is a deed used in many states to convey fee title to real property. Until the widespread use of title insurance, the warranties by the grantor were very important to the grantee. When title insurance is purchased, the warranties become less important as a practical means of recovery by the grantee for defective title.

WEAR AND TEAR: A term used to indicate the normal damage inflicted on a property through every-day use.

WELL INSPECTION: An official inspection of the water quality and functionality of a well system.

This is sometimes a required inspection for a closing in some States.

ZONE: A specific area within a municipality or other jurisdiction which conforms to certain guidelines regarding the use of property in the zone. Typical zones include single-family, multi-family, industrial, commercial and mixed-use.

Useful Links & References

৵৽৻

Foreclosure Laws by State:

www.realtytrac.com/foreclosure-laws/foreclosure-laws-comparison

Online Legal Websites for Real Estate forms:

Legal Zoom

www.legalzoom.com

Rocket Lawyer

www.rocketlawyer.com

Law Depot

www.lawdepot.com

Nolo

www.nolo.com

U.S. Legal Forms

www.USLegalForms.com

Legalwiz

www.legalwiz.zom

Resources for Selling a Land Contract:

Amerifunds

www.amerifunds.us

Mortgage Note Buyer US

www.mortgagenotebuyer.us

Cash Flow Connection Pro LLC

www.cashflowconnectionpro.net

Credit Report:

Annual Credit Report

www.annualcreditreport.com

My Fico

www.MyFICO.com

Credit Repair Information:

Federal Trade Commission Consumer Information on Credit Repair: www.consumer.ftc.gov

Reports on Credit Repair:

www.BankRate.com

Acknowledgements

This book was originally written in 2007, yet I never published it. It was born from the bright ideas I had when I first entered the business of Real Estate in 2006. I was so enthusiastic about helping people to become home owners; I wanted to share my new found knowledge. I wrote this book from a fresh point of view, and compiled everything I learned from my initial interviews and first twelve months of interaction with lenders, appraisers, home inspectors, and other Realtors in the profession.

Over the years I have edited this book at least a dozen times, and it sat on my hard drive waiting for a day when I would decide it was complete and release it. Although much has changed since I first got into the business, and within the first year I was in real estate, the sub-prime loan market crashed and property values began their slide down a slippery slope to the values we see today across the country.

As the dust has settled, and I have re-visited this book in a new unit of time, I discovered that it only needed minor editing to bring it up to date. Much of the information within it was unchanged, despite all the market changes.

The primary reason for this is that these principles presented here are basic. They are the fundamentals of finding your way into becoming a homeowner, and they all still work today as they did five years ago. One can follow these steps and become a homeowner, and achieve the American Dream.

Throughout the compilation of this book, I would have to say there are many people to acknowledge.

To begin, I want to thank my wife Margarita for her constant re-reading of the text over and over again from the viewpoint of a reader. Her expertise as an editor has few equals. Her patience is immeasurable.

Many thanks to my step-daughter: Juana

Salamanca who gave me the idea for the glossary so long ago.

I also want to thank my Broker, Al Morehart for the original inspiration many years ago to reach out and help renters become homeowners.

A special thanks to all the REALTORS® and staff at Troxel Realty Co. LLC, as well as the membership of the Battle Creek Area Association of REALTORS®. A truly amazing group of wonderful people!

Finally I want to thank my father for his wit and wisdom. His courage, grace and down-to-earth common sense have been the greatest instruction a son could ever ask for.

During the time I wrote this original manuscript, my mother Lucille H. Delaware passed away after a long struggle with cancer. From my earliest childhood, she always encouraged me to help others, as well as fulfill my dreams. This book is dedicated in her memory.

Now take this material, and apply it and go fulfill your dreams...

ABOUT THE AUTHOR

     Michael Delaware is a Phoenix, Arizona native who now resides in Battle Creek, Michigan with his wife Margarita. He also lived in Georgia for 15 years in the 1980's and 1990's where he owned and operated a stained and beveled glass studio in the Metro-Atlanta area. During those years he was an active volunteer in the community, coordinating annual Arts and Crafts Festivals in the downtown district of Roswell, Georgia. He also participated in Arts & Crafts Shows for over 25 years as a vendor in numerous States.   He has been a Michigan resident since 1999.

His other published works include numerous non-fiction books on real estate, sales management, marketing and other self-help topics. He has also published fiction and non-fiction stories for children

As an illustrator and photographer, he has included his works in his own books and blogs. He enjoys hiking and mountain biking in the great outdoors and taking long walks in the woods with his dog.

Currently he is an active Realtor in Michigan and frequent community volunteer. He is a member of the National Association of Realtors, The Council of Residential Specialists, and the Michigan Association of Realtors. He is also an active member of the Battle Creek Area Association of Realtors where he was awarded 'Realtor of the Year' in 2010, and served as Board President in 2011. He founded his own independent publishing company in 2012.

To follow Michael:

www.MichaelDelaware.com
Facebook.com/MichaelDelawareAuthor
Amazon.com/Author/MichaelDelaware
Linkedin.com/in/MichaelDelaware
@MichaelDelaware

Other titles by the author available as eBooks:

The Art of Sales Management: Lessons Learned on the Fly *(also available in paperback)*

The Art of Sales Management: Revelations of a Goal Maker *(also available in paperback)*

The Art of Sales Management: 75 Training Drills to Build Confidence, Excellence & Teamwork *(also available in paperback)*

Small Business Marketing: An Insider's Collection of Secrets *(also available in paperback)*

Arts & Craft Shows: The Top 10 Mistakes Artist Vendors Make... And How to Avoid Them! *(also available in paperback)*

Arts & Craft Shows: 12 Secrets Every Artist Vendor Should Know *(also available in paperback)*

Inspiration: The Journey of a Lifetime

For Real Estate:

Understanding Land Contract Homes: In Pursuit of the American Dream *(also available in paperback)*

Land Contract Homes for Investors *(also available in paperback)*

In Children's Fiction:

Scary Elephant Meets the Closet Monster

In Children's Non-Fiction:

My Name is Blue: The Story of a Rescue Dog

More titles will be available in print in late 2013 and in 2014. For a current list of available print books visit:

www.ifandorbutpublishing.com

If you found this book on real estate useful, you might also like these other titles by the same author:

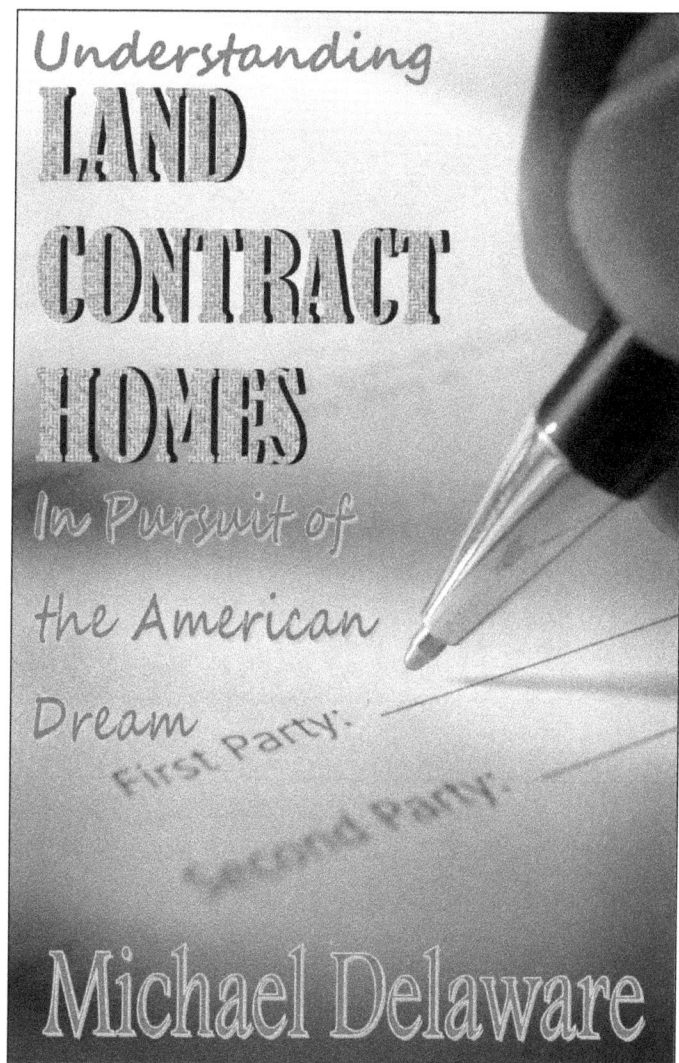

Understanding
LAND
CONTRACT
HOMES
In Pursuit of the American Dream

First Party.

Second Party.

Michael Delaware

Land Contract Homes

For Investors

Michael Delaware

If, And or But
Publishing Company

www.IfAndorButPublishing.com

www.ingramcontent.com/pod-product-compliance
Lightning Source LLC
Chambersburg PA
CBHW020153200326
41521CB00006B/355